Kniv[illegible]
Spo[illegible]ns

A chef's story of kitchens, addictions and mayhem

Alasdair Gill

MACMILLAN

First published 2026 by Macmillan
an imprint of Pan Macmillan
The Smithson, 6 Briset Street, London EC1M 5NR
EU representative: Macmillan Publishers Ireland Ltd, 1st Floor,
The Liffey Trust Centre, 117–126 Sheriff Street Upper,
Dublin 1 D01 YC43
Associated companies throughout the world

ISBN 978-1-0374-0143-5 HB
ISBN 978-1-0374-0144-2 TPB

9 8 7 6 5 4 3 2 1

A CIP catalogue record for this book is available from the British Library.

Illustrations by Alasdair Gill

Typeset by Palimpsest Book Production Ltd, Falkirk, Stirlingshire
Printed and bound in the UK using 100% Renewable Electricity
by CPI Group (UK) Ltd

FSC www.fsc.org
MIX
Paper | Supporting responsible forestry
FSC® C116313

Knives and Spoons

For Arlo

A Chef,
Well-seasoned

contents

the kitchen food chain

The commis
Homo rookisis

A culinary baby cub, the wide-eyed apprentice. Easily confused as a startled meerkat in oversized Crocs. Loves to wear the kitchen's disposable paper hats that make them look like they're selling Krispy Kreme doughnuts. Will ask for ingredients already on their section.

Natural habitat: larder

The chef de partie
Bigdickus disgruntlus

The one and only workhorse of the kitchen, also known as a line chef. The chef de partie has earnt their space and will defend it like a fox protecting a wheelie bin. Often loud communicators; outspoken. Team players until they're not. They might cover your shift, but will definitely try to shag the waiter.

Weaknesses: thinks waiters want to shag them

The breakfast chef
Scramblius maximus

A rarer sighting is this reluctant inmate of the kitchen world. They don't want to be part of your 'kitchen family'; they want a reliable shift and a reason to leave at 2 p.m. Oddly, every single one is religious. They are the most un-chef-like chefs you'll ever meet and are usually in the role due to a need for structure, on account of having six kids and a mortgage.

Strengths: relentlessly reliable
Weaknesses: likely to be a serial killer

The sous chef
Secondus in commandus

The on-sight special unit. They only hold this position through talent or time and know every recipe, every supplier issue, every staff lie, every skeleton in every walk-in fridge. Often more hands-on than the head chef.

Pros: self-assigns more cig breaks
Cons: ego, less banter

The head chef
Dictator culinaris

Hugely varying in nature: either very hands-on with a great talent for commanding the battlefield or can struggle to make a decent beurre blanc any more due to rotas and gross profit percentages taking over. Often seen wearing Crocs in black leather as a sign of status.

Natural habitat: the pass/the office

The pastry chef
Precisis sugarbitch

The neurodivergent cousin of the chef de partie. Works in a fridge, speaks in grams, lives for lamination. Where the kitchen absolutely stops being about 'winging it'. Most likely could produce a line chef's dishes far better, but lacks any desire to trade their sterile lab for the dirty trenches.

Strengths: shortbread, maths
Weaknesses: social gatherings, small-cock jokes

The floor manager
Cuntus wankertits

Often spotted lecturing a KP on 'professionalism' while wearing a scarf indoors. A creature fuelled predominantly by passive aggression, micromanagement and flat whites. Pretends to understand what dough lamination is to fluff the image that they're a foodie connoisseur.

Natural habitat: drinking at the bar
Strengths: schmoozing, uber lux
Weaknesses: limited allies

The agency chef
Tempus mercenarius

A drifting kitchen temp hired by the hour, a breed that has surged profoundly since Brexit and Covid. A hired gun to ease understaffing; a culinary one-night stand. Arrives mid-service like a suspicious package in the post in unsullied clogs.

Strengths: often gets paid more than the sous per hour

Weaknesses: no fucking clue where anything is and mildly resented by all

The private chef
Clientele brownosius

Cooks for the rich, celebs and people who eat tiramisu off things it shouldn't be eaten off. Adaptable – can live out of a Ford Fiesta full of cling film and cleavers or on a 30-foot yacht, a transition similar from war dog to house cat. Can turn any marble kitchen into downtown Beirut with one pan. Usually rarely sighted.

Natural habitat: n/a
Strengths: the MacGyver of catering; can build a Michelin experience out of a rented Airbnb pan set
Weaknesses: morally negotiable

The KP (kitchen porter)
Greaseium scrubershits

The true backbone of the kitchen. Holds the entire operation together with Marigolds and rage – and the unsung hero of prep. When they're good, they're worth their weight in tips (which can be substantial) as they can be fleeting creatures.

Natural habitat: pot wash
Weaknesses: eczema

kitchen slang

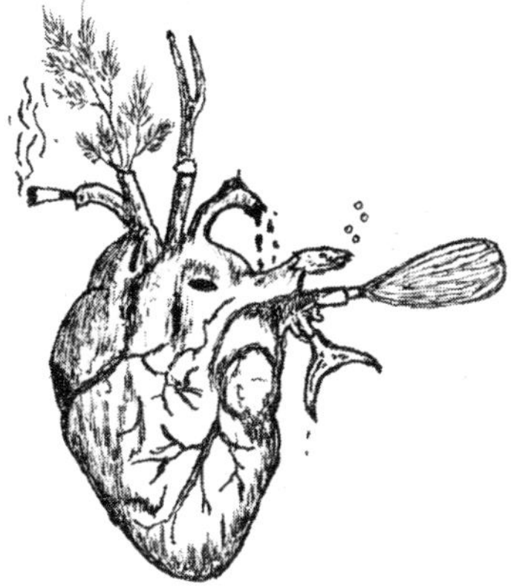

All day ***(awl-day)***

The total number of plates required from the tickets. The culinary equivalent of an accountant reading debt.

Dead space ***(ded-spayz)***

The void between lunch and dinner service where chefs either fall asleep upright or make catastrophically poor decisions in alleyways.

K-hole ***(kay-hohl)***

A by-product of dead space.

Drop it ***(drop-it)***

Cook – now and fast.

Emulsification ***(ee-MUL-sih-fih-KAY-shun)***

The careful blending of fat and liquid. Also, the state of kitchen morale – a thin, unstable suspension liable to split.

Fold ***(fohld)***

A gentle mixing technique that doubles as a physical, emotional and spiritual reaction from burnout.

Family meal ***(fam-uh-lee-meel)***

A communal meal prone to complaints before being demolished in thirty seconds by starved terriers.

Pan slam ***(pan-SLAM)***

A shock act of major rage. Also, levelling out an omelette.

More ***(maw)***

Gear; speedy powders. 'I'm gonna need some *more* asap'; 'Is there any *more* left?'

Service! ***(sur-viz)***

Get here!

Behind! ***(be-hynd)***

Get away!

Dead plate ***(ded playt)***

Get a clue.

Last orders ***(lahst or-duz)***

Get some 'more'.

Knob of butter ***(nob uv buhta)***

Measurement of a ping-pong ball. Or a playful reference to Chef's erectile dysfunction.

86 ***(ay-tee-siks)***

Done, finished, kaput, rejected, bin, get it out, bugger it off.

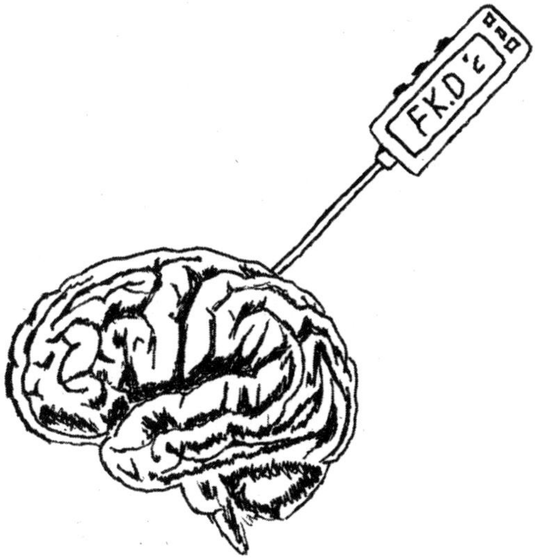

kitchen locations

Back of house (BOH)

The windowless kingdom where chefs spend most of their lives complaining, thriving, deteriorating, rolling up and sometimes hibernating.

Front of house (FOH)

The territory of waiters, bartenders and the three managers who materialise to fluff customers.

Larder section

Where you'll find cold starters, salads, oysters, shaky unsureness and everything else the seasoned chef doesn't want to deal with.

Walk-in

A fridge the size of a bedroom. Useful for emotions, poultry, temperature control, panic attacks and storing produce.

The pass

The final point of call between kitchen and waiter for a plate of food – unless deemed more worthy of the bin.

The line

The narrow strip of heated grills where chefs cook shoulder-to-shoulder like steamy sardines.

The pot wash

The wet zone. Home to the KP – a species forged in steam, sweat and industrial bleach. Approach in service with caution.

The nook

The cut-off dead space from the kitchen (see chapter 1).

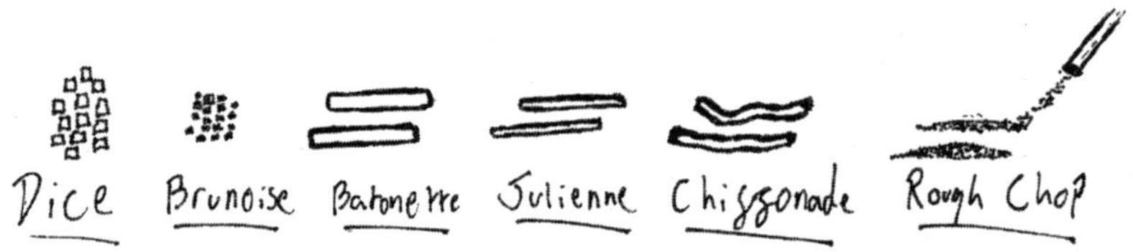

preface

Mise en place (meez-on-plahs)
Setting up. Preparation. Everything in place.

Heard it, you hungry little tourist?

'Yes, Chef!' The battle cry of amateurs and influencers, and the slogan on your dad's novelty apron come BBQ season.

Mise, though, is the real sacred culinary shibboleth. It's a chef's premeditation: the necessary ritual, the culinary foreplay that decides whether service grants a smooth climax or a *ménage à trois* that got out of hand between you, a blunted knife and 120 ravenous covers demanding satisfaction. You can clock a chef worth their salt by their *mise* within seconds. It's the way their station looks like a crime scene organised by a psychopath with boundaries. It's the calm. It's the economy of movement. The shallot striped, first into fine julienne and then into a finer *brunoise* so clean it could sanitise.

It's like watching an actor smoke on screen – something that's unactable. Real smokers move with a cigarette like it's an extra knuckle. You can't fake that comfort with a vice. It isn't a prop. It's anatomy.

Mise is the same. It's not a technique. It's a tell. It's a map of habit, trauma, hard-earned shortcut and superstition that a chef has ever had. And, no, it's not because they're clean freaks. It's actually the contrary. It's because they're seasoned enough through services that have gone absolutely tit over Croc from a lack of it. It's wisdom spawned from trauma, like armouring up because your fingers are down to single digits, or becoming authoritarian with wrapping up, knowing you're one itchy crotch away from a raw meat hazard.

I don't believe kitchen prep is an intuitive instinct buried deep in most chefs' DNAs.

If anything, it's violently at odds with the kind of people who end up in kitchens.

Most of us didn't plan to be here; we fell through the cracks and landed on a cutting board. We're creatures of impulse – nomadic, semi-feral runts stitched together with nicotine, burn scars and whatever coping mechanism didn't croak us last week.

Mise en place has to be beaten in, like bad habits out of a racehorse. Planning ahead? I've never been the type to do something today with the slightest ebb of awareness there might be a tomorrow. 'Everything in its place' is a kitchen teaching that no other intuition could get into me.

That probably doesn't sound like the opening confession of a breakthrough culinary prodigy. And it shouldn't; that's not me. I don't have a restaurant. I don't run the pass at a capital hotspot with a six-month waiting list and a PR team.

Those books do already exist and they're brilliant. Go read a Rick Stein or *White Heat* if you want the holy scriptures – although if it's not a 'one-or-the-other', I'm happy to place the culinary bar for you before Marco Pierre-White.

Writing about chefs is an awkward exercise: too close, too personal, too wordy, unnatural. Chefs writing anything themselves is worse. I'm not doing this from a calm desk with a herbal tea and a creative grant. I'm typing between jobs, with beetroot-stained knuckles and unfinished thoughts, Merlot reducing behind me, eyes still slightly vibrating from finishing at 3 a.m. after feeding a private party of eighty.

◆ ◆ ◆

Chefs are the people I admire, envy, resent, root for and, occasionally, fantasise about watching slip on a wet-floor sign and face-plant into their own hand blender. They are my people – the fiercest team players on earth and, at the same time, the finest crabs in a bucket that evolution has ever produced. We bleed for each other on service, then instinctively drag down anyone who crawls an inch higher to the light, purely because it wasn't us. It's a grotesque, beautiful collision of camaraderie and ego, generosity and spite, that would have fascinated Darwin enough to trade the Galápagos islands for a gastro pub pass any day.

If this book has a purpose, it's an overdue *mise en place* for a life in which I spent years with zero prep for a tomorrow that I believed was nothing but a wasted off-cut, a rumour, a conspiracy to be racked up, sniffed away and hocked onto the cold sidewalk like yolky phlegm.

If *mise* is the art of getting your shit together before the chaos, then this is perhaps an attempt to get mine in place before the next dish hits the pass.

If you're already smoothing out the dog-eared receipt for this book, preparing to return it, then no hard feelings. That's the point. There are far more of us than the world ever sees – the everyday chefs with long shifts, raw skin, sore knees, crooked spines, empty wallets, unbeatable vices and lives that look like a walk-in after an under-staffed Saturday service. We're alive on the outside and often incredibly simple seeming – and yet endlessly complex on the inside and rarely at peace.

This isn't about the greats. They're already canonised.

It's for the rest – the quiet backbones sweating it out, numbing something, moving furiously out of necessity to cease drowning and being convincing in their statement that they're under control; the ones who know exactly how to run a service and absolutely fuck-all about running a life.

For those still suffering, inside and outside the kitchen.

Consider this my *mise en place.*

Knives up. Spoons out.

Let's cook.

1

Drunk beef with whipped Roquefort and port reduction

Drunk Beef, Whipped Roquefort, Port Reduction

Serves / 20–30 canapes

Time / 20 mins + overnight

Ingredients

1. 500gr Beef fillet
½ Bottle Port
Boquet Garni – Thyme, Bay, Rosmary

Dressing

2. 100gr Marscapone
150gr Roquefort cheese
50ml double cream

4. 2–3 tbsp Caster Sugar

☆ Freeze before slicing

☆ It will spit when searing – Pat dry + air out

6. Oil for Searing
Chives / Shallot for Serving
Dehydrated baguett slices / wonton spoon for Serving

1. Marinade trimmed fillet with Port + herbs for 5hrs – overnight. Sealed + Fridge

☆ 2. Whipped Roquefort – beat marscapone first, then Roquefort. Cream to loosen

3. Port reduction – once fillet is marinaded, take out from port, pat dry with paper towel, then back into fridge uncovered for hour.

4. Reduce port on med-high heat with sugar til thick + syrupy.

Crackle. My roll-up hissed as I dragged it to life, the little white rock nestled inside blistering like hot oil on pork skin. Chemical smoke curled past my rouge-, garlic- and port-stained fingers. I froze to hold my breath, counted silently, forcing it deeper into my wheezy lung – a false desperation for more potency.

A thick plume of chemical smoke unravelled as I exhaled. My consciousness was unpressed, like someone had released their steel-capped boot from inside my skull. Palms grew clammy as my jaw clamped firmer. I didn't just feel the blood rushing to my face, I could hear it, crashing and swarming upward, a reverse waterfall, a stampede surging from body to skull.

I clambered to my feet and buttoned up my chef's jacket.

Every shift here started in the nook (*No-ok*) – a sweet spot in every kitchen and something they don't teach you about in Cordon Bleu; a drastic change from the atmospheric temperature and the heat of the grills. For many kitchens, the nook might be a small space in dry storage or a walk-in fridge. Maybe an odd L-design nether zone that feeds around to the pot wash. But it's part of every kitchen's anatomy, like a lung that breathes, roars and chokes. And it's a remedy to the adrenaline that thrives in the very air around service time. It's a place of silence amid the cacophony of husky-voiced orders, the high-pitched clinks of saucepans, the baritone thuds of pots and all the orchestral trimmings of a restaurant in full swing.

If you're a pastry chef, you live in a nook. It's a luxurious one, a cool and calm sanctuary smelling of stilton and shortbread. Pastry chefs work to a different rhythm to the rest of the kitchen, a steady metronome keeping their own continuous beat alongside the manic, unpredictable jazz band they share a studio with. The energy and focus of the shift itself also leaves a very different mark on the pastry chef compared to their comrades in the rest of the kitchen. If a blind man poked his nose at each one of us, he would be sniffing the difference between a fresh pastel de nata with hints of vanilla versus a corpse fermenting in veal stock.

I'm not a pastry chef, not by breed. They are too professional, in the pernickety sense, for most line chefs: it's house cats versus stray dogs, contemporary fine art versus finger painting. The only exception is in a triple Michelin-starred kitchen. If you ever manage to dip your head in one, that's what most restaurants' pastry sections look like on a large scale – and their chefs too. But that's where any cross-pollination stops. Another big difference is that their pristine nooks are rarely used for passing out in or smoking crack.

Located in a late-night joint called the Plum Gate in London's East End, this was the most remarkable nook I'd ever sliced, diced or flambéed next to. The Plum was a long kitchen with a dip in the middle for the pot washers.

At the end of the kitchen pass was the nook, a concrete-bricked room about the area of a single parking space. Inside sat three odd chairs, a table with a plate and endless clutter on the ground: baggies, bottles, fag butts, lottery tickets, you name it. It was stale and smoky by day and a boozer coffin by night. It was a zen den in which to realign – a little nasal, liver and cranium spa where you could aggressively smoke, drink, scream, snort, crunch, pop and inhale all your systems back to regular. And it had a strict chef-only membership.

Never in my rocky career have I experienced such a drastic change in atmosphere than when crossing the threshold of the Plum's nook. No matter how loud the kitchen was, the second that the weighted nook door slammed behind you, there was near silence, with only a distant murmur from the bustling restaurant above.

It occupied a unique position in space and time, a place that felt like you had wandered off the end of the earth and checked out of life for a moment – but with pleasure.

I was twenty-six: unmanageable, unhinged, unreliable and predictably unpredictable. Showing up on time had become an endeavour beyond anything I was capable of promising. Days would begin any time, day or night, on stranger's floors, in doorways or on cold pavements, sometimes with splatters of blood, piss and cider – with the best-case scenario being that they all came from me.

I didn't know how to live. I'd never felt prosperous in anything: no drive, no passion, no awe for the future, no political views or clean clothes (nor any understanding of how to wash them). The belief that something different could possibly be on the cards was totally fanciful. There was no HR, no customer service, no beady-eyed cashier in a red velvet two-piece I could grab by the lapel and desperately plea, 'Cash in my chips. I want to exchange this life for a new one!'

I didn't live to work. I worked to use. Every penny earned on shift (and more) was spent on substances to get through the day. I was in debt – and not in an adult way. I owed money to everyone I knew: friends, family, corner shops, junkies, good people, assholes and every dealer in your phonebook.

Being by the grills may well have been a belonging, but I was in no space to appreciate that. The loud and chaotic kitchen was, ironically, the calmest place for my rattling mind. It was familiar, it made sense and I knew it well. Being momentarily distracted by getting the exact amount of pink from a thyme-crusted rack of lamb or trimming and blanching a duck breast to order felt like the last razor-thin strand holding me from an unknown abyss.

At a stretch, I could conclude that stints in a kitchen at least offered numbing breaks to the harrowing solitude and inconceivable boredom from using alone. Life felt stagnant, but that was naive; it was fermenting, and the permanent dirt I was spiralling down towards was unknowingly imminent.

◆ ◆ ◆

Mornings in the Plum's kitchen started lifeless. I'd stumble in for a shift either still high or looking so rough it could panic a late-stage terminal patient into insisting I take their seat, fluids included. On this particular morning, we had another private event. There were canapés to finish, a hangover to manage and, as always, existential dread to garnish. The chemical malaise was baked into my bones, lodged in my thoughts and encrusted thick across my tongue.

There's a strange kind of synergy between a chef and his kitchen when you're hanging out your arse from the night before. You walk into that cold, sterile room, the metallic counters gleaming like an abandoned operating theatre, and, for a moment, it mirrors you perfectly: lifeless, joyless, reeking faintly of death. Then, slowly, you start the ritual.

Ovens click. Vents hum. Grill up, stock order in. Pink Floyd bleeds from the party box speaker. Bit by bit, the place wakes up. Colour seeps back into the world; heat returns to the bones; body and kitchen both start to function again.

When the pulse finally steadies, I would head to the nook.

The nook has a little red nursery chair, a relic of unknown – and best unasked – origin. I unbuttoned my top whites, grabbed the blowtorch and relit my dry roll-up. The first exhale drifted out, not twenty minutes into opening, like a chef sighing at the end of a double shift. I swigged my Irish coffee and laid out the morning's *mise en place* – a plate dusted with two neat piles: coke on the left, ketamine on the right.

Through the vast à la carte of narcotics a day could hold, my set menu was fixed: cocaine, ketamine and Xanax – and not the prescription kind but those wonky, homemade knock-outs laced with fentanyl. That was the baseline, the fuel to face another day. Measuring the stuff had become unbearably dull. One without the other felt meaningless, like serving a bisque with no spoon or bowl. The result was predictable: my nose and mouth perpetually mangled, aggressively tenderised and awaiting a battering. Cheap gin and corner-shop cider blistered the inside of my cheeks, while the powders burnt through what was left of my sinuses.

But then, for a moment, a split second of chemical grace, the fog lifted. The noise stopped.

'Laarrrggghhh.' I froze in a blank stare, trying to make sense of the directionless noise.

Did that come from me?

It was the subconscious suffering of someone bleeding out

on a battlefield. Christ, even the voices in my head couldn't stand being there.

'Durrgggghhhh.'

No, it definitely wasn't in my head. The desperate gargle triggered my glance to catch sight of progressive movement under the vent. Clutter was shifting, bottles clinking as they slid to each side.

I froze.

A rat? Some kind of mutant kitchen monster brought forth by the chaos of the nook? A bright-red hand flung out of the mess and firmly gripped the venting shaft. It then proceeded to pull the rest of its anatomy to its shaky feet. No mutant rat, mangy fox or monster. Well, not entirely.

Karl, our head chef, had awakened from his slumber. His skinny legs were shakily unstable, while his skin was bright red with a visible leathery texture. Though he wasn't much older than me, in this moment he could have been a decade my senior. He looked at me with bloodshot, pinhead pupils, his gaze unfocused, and rapidly flicked his fingers back and forth like an elderly mute signalling for a change of briefs.

I handed him my cigarette and pickled coffee. He took a deep inhale, gulped until his eyes jittered back into his swollen scalp and finished with a burpy exhalation of smoke.

'Wooooof,' he croaked under husky vocal cords.

Sleeping in the nook wasn't an everyday occurrence but it happened, especially with Karl. Under his leadership, the kitchen had become the place to get even looser after a shift. Why would we need another place to go 'party' after work when we had a glorified ventilation cupboard full of baggies and cheap whisky, one that repelled any type of person you wouldn't want to drink with?

Karl snatched the nook plate and looked from me towards

the two mini mountains of fresh powder on each side of the dish.

'Which one?' he coughed out. I directed Karl's tooter to the coke.

We'd all seen terrible cock-ups when chefs, waiters, nook visitors and local tarts of both sexes thought they were snorting a booster of cocaine, only to realise with sudden dread they had inhaled something to open up the portals and take them to a different universe entirely. Shifts would stop and nannying would begin; simultaneous projectile vomiting along with vicious shitting through leather pants once occurred, all because of the wrong pile of powder.

Karl put a straw straight to the powdery mountain and honked his system back to artificial functionality. He loved cocaine, more than air; we all did, but Karl especially. Coke fuelled his workaholism like gas powers a grill. He indulged in downers too as a potential post-shift à la carte option.

As someone who loved to go up, he found my obsession to go down harder to watch. My own tolerance for downers had become so high that hits, topped up with the frequency of fag breaks, were barely touching the sides. Karl occasionally attempted limp interventions but, given his own predilections, it felt something like the steaming pot telling the kettle to sort its life out through an only slightly less powdered spout. On the whole, uppers were far more accepted in kitchens.

Mark, another chef de partie, entered the nook.

'Morning, crew. We need oil. The fryers are naked.'

He's a remarkable specimen and one of the most extreme drinkers I've ever had the pleasure of encountering. Without fail, Mark would arrive on shift with an empty two-litre bottle of Eastern European vodka, no matter what time of day it was. He had a croaking, battered voice and was covered in the most horrendous gashes and burns, all around his anatomy. Cooking pissed and being right on the edge of unconsciousness every day had made him look like he'd just done ten rounds with Freddy Krueger and was one blister from being an official burns victim.

Mark had previously been a chef offering up his culinary humanitarian aid services in some of the deadliest spots in the world whenever a war broke out. As a result, he suffered from PTSD and would shudder when pots were thrown too hard. Drowning himself in cheap spirits had become his chief way of coping with it all.

'My, teeth . . . they're greasy,' Mark croaked as he shuffled his tongue around his mouth.

'The toothpaste? It's done something,' he continued, confused. We had a little station of deodorant and gum, a paltry attempt at freshness after sweating chemicals for days. I paused in thought, just for a moment, before bursting into a slow cackle.

I knew exactly what he'd done . . . because, well, he'd actually done it before.

Karl, although a fast mover on the kitchen floor, would often carry a limp in his step. This was due to so much of his coked-fuelled anger being taken out bursting anal vessels on the crapper.

I divulged my theory to Mark.

'I think you've brushed your gnashers with head chef's haemorrhoid cream . . . again, Chef.'

Karl began to laugh.

'Oh . . . bugger,' Mark croaked, but then began to laugh drunkenly with me and Karl.

'Enough, it's go-time,' Karl declared as his eyes started to centre.

We fled the nook to the grills, while ping-ponging back and forth to ready our *mise en place.*

'Bass?'

'Filleted and de-boned.'

'Chicken tits?'

'Needed butterflying.'

'Jus?'

'Topping up now.'

'Lava cakes?'

'Working.'

'Canapés?'

'I'm on it, Chef.'

Though we use 'chef' as a catch-all term, there is a vast difference to who they are, what they're capable of, what jokes they can take and how likable they are. Cheffing must be the only job where half the workers turn down the top job when offered it. The second you become head chef, life becomes less about the food and more about spreadsheets and rotas. The whole reason we became line chefs is because we can't read, organise or multiply – or behave. Karl was the most hands-on head chef; the mad general on the battlefield.

Although at first glance you might look at him and wonder how the fuck this man had been allowed within fifty feet of a kitchen, let alone put in charge of one, he actually ran a terrifyingly tight shipwreck, with the sort of obsessive, militaristic efficiency you only develop after being traumatised by a Michelin demigod.

He'd been forged and lightly battered under Pierre Koffman. He still carried the scars, physical and emotional, of his time there. His least favourite memory? It was perhaps the funniest: being sent on a frantic hotel-wide hunt for the 'parsley curlers' – an obviously made-up tool invented purely for the sport of watching a young chef panic-sprint through every corridor like a demented bellhop.

Everyone was in on it: the KP, the bellboy, the maids – all gleefully watching him tear the place apart, looking for a fictional utensil. When he finally realised, the humiliation was catastrophic. He stormed out, torched every bridge in sight and vowed never to look stupid in a kitchen again.

◆ ◆ ◆

For that night's private function, it was corporate canapés and I was taking the reins on my section: wild mushroom and butternut arancini with tarragon aioli, tuna crudo with yuzu and dill, and, my little personal bite, the drunken beef – meat with an alcohol content. It was fine dining: refined and yet something totally caveman. A fillet was soaked in port overnight, seared and served carpaccio-style with a swivel of whipped Roquefort and a syrupy port reduction from the same bath the meat had been marinating in. A clever and rich little bite, holding a unique balance.

We all went to our stations as the Plum sailed forward towards service. That's how it goes at the beginning: dysfunctional functionality, with the team finding a kind of queasy equilibrium. I got into the zone for a couple of hours after the drunken fillet and focused on the dull, all-consuming task of rolling out vast amounts of arancini. I started them and then the second I saw Viv, the KP, free from pots, I passed to her and ducked for cover.

Viv was half-Italian, half-Eastern European and did a startlingly convincing cosplay of the queen from *Snow White* in full witch mode. If there was ever a long hair to be found, it could only have come from a growth on her face; and when she grinned at us, she displayed her blackened teeth, easily countable on one hand. She was our trusty KP, as in she sprayed and washed our mess with an anger fuelled by an inner rage that this was her life. Anything new that needed polishing was met with screaming profanities about our mothers that needed Google Translate to understand. We often played a high-stakes game of Buckaroo with her, like petty schoolboys: how heavily you dared place something in her sink without her throwing it back as she cursed an army of Sardinian sausages on your mother.

But, an hour in, our *mise en place* was interrupted by the arrival of the brand-new floor manager, Kevin.

The Plum had been without a manager for a couple of months now, after it had been discovered that the last manager had stolen tens of thousands of pounds from the company and was now on the run.

Kevin was a middle-class, preppy bloke – and painfully posh. He was an extracurricular kind of guy, that strange breed of Brit who adored stout and was oddly into the royals. Though only in his early thirties, he presented as much older and clearly had never cleared a table, mopped a floor or shagged anything that was easily confusable with an aquatic mammal.

I hold a low degree of sympathy for any new outsourced floor manager starting out, but there was some pity in the mix that day, nonetheless. You were starting a job with a team that already mildly despised you as you told veteran workers to do their job differently while learning the ropes yourself.

Kevin approached the pass with an anxious purpose. 'Morning, chefs!' he announced at volume.

At best, a low murmur was returned with no eye contact from any of us, not even Karl who was practically facing him on the other side of the pass. It wasn't exclusively ill-mannered; the kitchen was busy and we were all working hard at our stations.

Kevin reached a hand to turn down the kitchen speaker that was blasting techno.

'I said, "Good morning, chefs!"'

The kitchen froze as chemical-ridden brains attempted to configure what had happened. A full-grid power cut or the airwaves clearing for a nuclear announcement seem more fathomable than the reality of someone having the salt to manhandle our Party Rocker 3000.

'How about we tune down that gay-boy techno?' Kevin snorted, in an attempt to try and communicate at what he believed was our level. 'No wonder it's a pussy-free zone here!'

He thought he was speaking our language, just as how men who went to public school suddenly get a hint of Ray Winstone in their voice when asking a builder if they fancy a 'cuppa.'

Perhaps, in Kevin's mind, the homophobic jest would earn him some respect.

Now, I'd be lying if I said that kind of chat didn't happen in kitchens, but what Kevin clearly didn't know was that Karl was a very easily triggered, closeted bisexual. Our last chef de partie was literally chased out of a full restaurant by Karl gripping a cleaver for not believing, out of grotesqueness, that a male steward had a three-hour layover in Karl's rear the previous night.

'Now, I want to start on the right foot with you all. My job here is to manage. And manage I shall!' Kevin continued.

Karl's gaze slowly rose from his emulsion and landed firmly on Kevin's damp acne-ridden face.

'You see, guys, things are going to change around here. I can't pretend that I didn't see when I went into your little nook at the back.'

Karl's eyes were widening with every word coming out of Kevin's mouth, blood now visibly rushing to his usually pasty face in silent rage.

'What have you got to say to this?' Kevin presented his phone screen that showed a picture of our powdery nook plate caked with narcotics.

I couldn't believe it. None of us could.

How fucking dare he? Who was this guy? Furious entitlement swarmed my head while a thought protruded: *Are we all in trouble?* No, it's just a bit of gear. Is that such a crime? Maybe. He might have told the police; he looks like a tell-the-teacher kind of guy. The more I thought of it, this could be horrific.

While trying to make sense of this alien interaction, I could feel the rage emanating off Karl, like steam whistling out of a boiling pressure pot. There was something about the picture that felt so personally invasive. Kevin might as well have showed us a picture he took last night, spreading Karl's arse cheeks as he was passed out under the vents.

The vessels in Karl's forehead began visibly pulsing. You could bet with some certainty that a fresh haemorrhoid was blossoming on his sphincter in that very moment. Even Viv, the feistiest, foul-mouthed, communist-loving pot washer who would most likely survive a nuclear apocalypse and who understood not a word of English, let a damning 'Ooo cazzo' out of her toothless mouth in astonishment for Karl's manhood.

Chef's predatory pupils began to gaze past the now-trembling phone and to lock with piercing intensity into what looked like Kevin's soul.

In that moment of silence, it seemed to dawn on our new manager that he was in fact in acute danger. The moment almost had a flavour to it: you could taste it in the air, bitter but curiously moreish. Kevin clearly thought he was coming here to deal with a couple of dandy pastry chefs who would be mortified by the reality of being confronted by their plate of powders. Wrong. Kevin was now in uncharted territory with totally foreign rules. He had waltzed into the As-Salam Palace in Baghdad to declare there were going to be some changes around here, before giving a double-handed smack to the arse of Saddam's favourite wife.

Kevin began to take half a pace back, his whole anatomy reconfiguring from predator to prey. Karl remained deafeningly silent as his hawk-eyed stare remained fixed ahead. And then – BANG. Both of Karl's fists hit the pass with a furious thud, shaking his entire section.

Kevin's primal instinct took over his shaky legs and he bolted, fleeing up the stairs like a baby gazelle before a pride of famished leopards.

We heard him emit a panicked squeal, one that he'd probably never even heard himself make, as Karl hopped over the pass and tore after his new manager with white-knuckled fists pumping, jaw locked, and frothing at the mouth with coke-laced indignation. He was a man with no plan beyond catching up with Kevin and confronting him, but he was so viciously triggered that his body bolted faster than his logic, which never stood a fucking chance.

The nerve. Karl was an unhinged kind of leader whose life had felt so reductive, due to over-fermenting in the lethal combo of inadequacy and cocaine, that he didn't care how many days he had left in his bunker.

Kevin came in, as many managers do, as a NATO force – overseeing, overbearing and ultimately unclear as to exactly what it can really do in foreign territory. Roles like that can only work their authority when the kitchen has the head chef of a loud but bite-less power. Kevin had strolled into the Kremlin, declared himself leader and tied it off by calling Putin a little puff.

Viv began cackling, as if she'd finally got Snow White to munch the apple.

'Ritardato mentale!' she croaked. Google Translate wasn't needed.

The kitchen continued, as if someone had pressed pause on a movie for a second to deal with a heckler. I finished the whipped Roquefort, packed it into a piping bag and turned off the hob for my reduction, which was showing a deep-rouge gloss, boasting thick syrupy bubbles that domed and burst in slow motion. I poured the remaining port that the drunken beef fillet had been sitting in all night into two tin mugs. Mark and I clinked, smirked and drunk the cold, oaky nectar with deep meaty undertones before 'checking on the pastries'. We slumped ourselves on the beaten chairs of the nook, both thinking about what we'd just witnessed.

As the acidic port swept Mark's tongue, he began to finger the inside of his lips in bemusement.

'Sharp on the tongue?' I questioned.

He turned in wide-eyed astonishment. 'It's sorted my mouth blisters! Chef's anus toothpaste! It's cured me!'

We heard the leaps and scuttles from above as our head chef chased the new floor manager out the building.

Mark exhaled. 'Can you believe that bloody asshole?'

I wasn't sure if he was referring to Kevin or to Karl's blistering haemorrhoids. It didn't matter.

We clinked mugs again anyway, letting the hallowed comfort of the nook swallow us again. Service would start soon. Chaos would return.

Our *mise en place* was set: a nicotine-scorched bunker, a dusty chemical plate, mental outbursts and just enough camaraderie to maintain the apathy to do it all again.

2

Crab linguine with chilli, fennel and lemon

Crab linguine

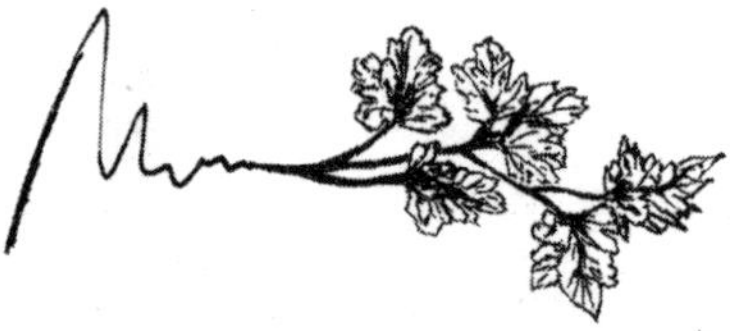

Serves 4-6 ppl

☆ Capellini / Angel hair

Prep - 10
Cook - 15

Ingredients

1. { 1 tbsp fennel seed — Toasted
2 small red chilli — deseeded + diced
2 garlic cloves }

3. { 150gr brown meat
300gr White meat
1 tbs Creme fraiche — easily double
2 large lemons — 1 for finish }

☆ Brown then White on low not to cook further

5. { 500gr linguine
Parsley
Chervil }

6. { Fennel fronds
Salt + peps
Olive oil — Garnish generously }

☆ 1 Toast fennel seeds - Make paste with chilli + garlic in pestle + Mortar

2. Cook on wide pan for couple mins on low with olive oil — No Colour

3. Add brown first - let melt in for a min then build + season - 1 lemon (zest + juice), White meat, Creme fraiche

Finishing school was like closing a book I'd never read. A decade before the Plum Gate, I'd blindly folded as the cliché that got kicked out more times than attended – for generally existing in all ways that didn't fit the syllabus. And when it was officially over, I stood there, naked in the open, like a plucked pigeon at a vegan deli, totally un-hireable. Everyone seemed to have the next chapter neatly printed out: universities, apprenticeships, gap years in Tanzania. I didn't even have the table of contents. I was missing something; a blueprint to life had got lost in the post.

By some miracle, I landed a job at The Delaunay, which was forged by a kind of London restaurant royalty. It was a grand, Parisian-style brasserie with a hint of Hungarian and Swiss precision. I started as a barista and these became some of the most important few months of my life.

I did it, of course, as a means – cash, so I could run away – but somewhere between polishing silver and burning milk, I reluctantly fell in love; with the rhythm, the chaos, the trust and the romance of fine dining: the late nights, the clatter of cutlery, the snooty customers, the quiet satisfaction when service lands just right.

For the first time, I was relied upon and I was good at it, being part of a team that ran on adrenaline and through hangovers. I felt burnt out and it was a godsend. I learned the gospel of hospitality – late finishes, unholy starts, immaculate service – and, maybe most importantly, I finally had something on my CV other than 'kicked out'.

◆ ◆ ◆

I fled to Asia, wandered for months, rode around, worked in a bar, got arrested for opium possession, spent some nights in a Laos prison cell. I eventually returned, reluctantly, at square one. Or nearly. Thanks to the stint at The Delaunay, I landed a job at a Michelin-starred restaurant in west London. I was hired to polish glasses, but within a week I'd been moved to back of house, exiled for my long, knotted hair and my inability to iron a shirt. I was, apparently, polluting the open-plan ambience worse than a podgy northerner at a Chelsea reformer pilates class. I was out of sight – scrubbing dishes, clearing gutters, polishing glassware – but I didn't mind. It was, in fact, instant relief.

The work became an odd kind of salvation. I resented it, but it was keeping me steady. Being forced into exhaustion – bone-tired from labour again – was its own quiet ecstasy. Finishing at 2 a.m. and starting again a few hours later, the rhythm became a strange form of balance.

This was my first taste working as a prep chef: scrubbing fat off the sliding floor, hosing down the endless oily dishes and taking out the gargantuan rubbish bags just as they verged on splitting an entire eco system all over the floor. The steps into handling food happened quickly, but this was by no means down to me being a shining prodigy. It was more that there are endless mundane jobs in the kitchen that most chefs are happy to hand over to a lobotomised orangutan.

◆ ◆ ◆

I diced herbs with a mezzaluna, peeled the rainbow carrots, sliced and trimmed the Amalfi lemon. I'd never felt produce like that. What a pernickety revelation, to know it was possible to fuck up a carrot's colour by peeling it too far, or to discover what a lemon was meant to look like. They were huge and a whole new shade of yellow. Really fucking yellow – vivid and saturated. You could smell their tantalising, sweet acidic tang before even seeing them.

I'd just begun flattening out the white crab flesh, picking out small bits of shell by prodding slowly every corner and crevice. It felt obscene at first, filtering the crab centimetre by centimetre. Then, this one day, as the shift rolled from service to prep, I was zesting the endless yellow Amalfi mountain on my section when, from behind, I got my first 'Oi!'

My eyes darted up from my small corner of a station, freezing on the blank wall inches in front of me at the unmistakable shriek of a pissed-off sous chef. There were half a dozen chefs, busboys and waiters swarming around, all potential contenders for the terrifying end-of-lunch shriek. But, somehow, you just know when it's for you. It cut past them all, down the grills, over the pastry, through the pass and landed bang in my spine like a weighted cleaver.

'Oi, Ponytail! Come here!'

Oh, for fuck's sake, I hate this ponytail. So embarrassing – I've only tied it up for them. No one would choose to look like a semi-pro slackliner selling dry hash.

'Now!' he followed up with impressive volume.

'Coming,' I squeaked back, trying to match his impressive high volume, but just heightening the pitch instead.

I glided over to the grills in a cold panic while consciously trying my best to look calm. A half-run, half-walk took over, resulting in a bizarre low-lunging canter to the grills.

The sous chef, Dave, had tossed linguine in a pan and didn't even lift his gaze to look at me. He was tall, dark-haired and a bloke's bloke. He looked like a Dave. The most Dave thing was his beard; it was an intentional beard, one that was just plainly unachievable for most guys. It was remarkably bushy but trimmed, dark, oiled and purposeful.

Underneath his facial forest of testosterone was an eerily expressionless face, making his loud orders and presence more terrifying. There was a total lack of ability to read where he was at. It was almost reptilian – cold and focused.

Kitchens are full of jokes, banter and treading the line of HR. How do I know if he fancied having a laugh about my mum or whether he was ready to feed my ponytail through the pasta machine?

'Look, here. What's that?' He spoke firmly while pointing up to the ceiling. I looked up in bemusement at the beige roof, wondering what exactly I should call it. Surely he didn't want me to say 'the ceiling'. The canopy? That sounds cleverer, though maybe incorrect. The lightbulb?! Ah, the lights! One of them was slightly flickering, but, again, were they actually lights? They were kinda abstract. Pendants, maybe.

As I gazed at the ceiling with an airy nonchalance, out of the corner of my eye I saw his stone-set face turn to me.

'Here, you tit!'

He pinned his vision to the tip of his finger, where my dopey eyes finally focused on a tiny orange and white shard, the tip of a little crab pincer.

With only a small wince of relief, solely because I now knew what was happening, I started to stutter, 'Oh, that. I was on crab . . . but can't have . . . you see it must be the . . .'

'I don't care,' he spat, halting my warm-up of excuses, like he'd lived this whole situation a hundred times before.

'A fuck-up is what it is. This right here isn't a linguine. In this dish is hours of prep, sweat, time, missed family and dedication. This little shell fucks it all. This little shell stops someone walking away thinking about the flavours of their meal. This fucking shell crunched their tooth and cut their mouth. Do better.'

Do better. That was probably the meaning of the Sanskrit tattoo on his neck.

It's a fair point, if not a tad toe-curling. Dave wiped the shell on my apron as a dismissal, like a playground alpha swiping his snot on the weak, and I returned to my station with my ponytail between my legs. More than anything, I was just relieved for the confrontation to be over. Being on the spot was truly horrific, it felt as if I was getting told off on stage in front of an audience wincing silently. It felt so personally triggering and familiar, like I'd lived variations of exactly that my entire life. My whole existence has felt, for the most part, just like one big bollocking, a frustrated call from every angle of authority to 'do better, focus, try harder', from teachers, family, girlfriends, police officers – and now beardy bloody chefs called Dave.

The shift was up: I packed up, wiped down and buggered off.

One of the best things about the place were the family meals – how they fed us. The full menu was left out in pots, like a rustic, fine-dining buffet, after every shift. Anyone who's done a decent round of hospitality will tell you how much of a luxury this is, particularly as some of the starters' prices here edged towards three digits.

The second that massive clock hit 5 p.m., I steamed over to pack in a box of pear tart, a couple of farinata and, of course, my treasured crab linguine. At least it felt like mine. It was an iconic and yet simple dish, holding so few ingredients that half of them were chopped, sliced and poorly picked by me. It felt personal; my contribution to lunchtime service.

I jolted out to the back exit, swiping a bottle of house red while doing so.

Outside, Jay was waiting for me with his guitar, which he often did after a shift so we could go on to our next establishment together.

◆ ◆ ◆

Jay and I had met in line at McDonald's at three in the morning when we were sixteen, both freshly expelled from our latest schools with no future plans. I had a Smartie-sized nug of squashed hash; he had half of a torn fag. It was the beginning of our long, symbiotic relationship and we were inseparable from then on, like two broken halves clogging an unfillable hole. Music, girls, style, insecurities . . . We were the same. Our only difference was that, although we both played guitar in a band, Jay could actually play. More than play, in fact. His was effortless raw talent, once-in-a-generation stuff. He could make bits of money with it and I couldn't. So his fingers smelt of brass, mine of crab.

Our big bond that set us apart from others was that we didn't want to just get high like our peers. We wanted to get so clinically lobotomised that we'd be eligible for a blue parking permit. We weren't into sipping and sniffing. We sought drowning and suffocating. It was anything, everything – and all of it all the time. Life was so painfully ordinary that nothing felt more exciting than the prospect of something making us feel different. But, at sixteen, it was predominantly cheap hash, cut coke, stolen booze and deodorant. Until we found Mental Matt and Misty River.

Misty River Hotel, a six-storey Georgian establishment sandwiched between embassies and overlooking the pristine verdant lawn of Kensington Gardens, was my first intro to hospitality. From a distance, Misty River looked grand due to its stature and its pristine neighbours, but as you neared, its unkept, tired and flaky exteriors became apparent.

Walking in was a jolt to all senses, but mainly smell. An overwhelming chemical stench sat stagnantly in the stale, cluttered space and, if it was particularly bright and sunny outside, your vision would go jet black for a few seconds as your eyes adjusted to the eerily dim, dingy and unoccupied reception.

As you may be concluding, Misty River didn't have a Michelin star and was perhaps the polar opposite to the bright-coloured, high-end restaurant I spent the other half of my time in. Misty River was not a place of respectable hospitality, but one of the largest drug dens north of the river. Through my years of crack dens, squats, shacks, penthouses and basements, I've never come close to the debauched chaos on such a grand scale than that found at Misty River. The establishment belonged to a totally broken, drug-dependent family that, by hiding in plain sight, had somehow survived the odds of not getting nicked.

Mental Matt was the youngest of the family. In his mid-twenties, he was a larger-than-life character who would often go get his morning pizza down Kensington High Street wearing just torn underwear and dribbling a football between his jet-black feet. He earnt about 90 per cent of the hotel's income from selling every drug you can think of out of his lair in the basement. Everything except, proudly, heroin.

Dealing with junkies was a tiresome part of Matt's life and it rattled him having to grow up around the by-product of, well, a junkie family. He was into speedier things and didn't suit the downer. His personality was a loud presence primed to holding court – fearless and utterly hilarious. His mother Elfie worked out of the attic and was one of the most prolific crack dealers in London. Small, slow-moving and pale as a ghost's arse in moonlight, she had the most remarkable crooked neck I've ever seen, bent at such a right angle that when she limped around, it looked like an overly dramatic audition for *Richard III*.

Elfie would beg, poke and whine profusely to Matt every day for more – more cash, more drugs, more anything, because, as it turned out, net profits are far more of a feat as a crack dealer if you're also a smoker. Between Matt in the basement and Elfie in the attic were dozens of worn-out rooms hosting bespoke lawlessness – the full spectrum of sex, drugs and rock 'n' roll, far less glamorous than the song but still tantalisingly exciting. That's where I spent most of my teens with Jay. It didn't seem for a moment like this was a grim den full of trouble, but a fucking fast pass to Disneyland.

Being sixteen, Matt was adamant that Jay and I never went upstairs to his mum. It was his half-hearted attempt at looking out for us. He became a sort of big brother, mentor and dealer, but mostly a vending machine. From the get-go, he'd hand us whatever else his little corner shop offered: coke, pills, DMT and enough acid to travel for months without leaving the room. He even let us run up absurd tabs that he knew we'd never pay off.

But he kept warning us off the real business upstairs – the pipes and the needles. For him, it was sacred territory, off-limits. For us, it was an open chicken coop and we were a couple of terriers. It didn't take long. We sprinted up those stairs the first chance we got. We found the gear and learned the rituals and sat in the dusty attic that stank, from two floors down, of smack and piss – which, if you don't know, are the two smells that always come together. It's an easy one to remember. Maybe piss without brown. But never brown without piss.

Nobody really has many morals in those places. They showed us how to cook with spoons and how to smoke it right.

We kept it secret from Matt for a bit, but word eventually got to him. In one way, it was a plus; he now felt allowed to smoke with us – guilt-free – his main addiction: 'spicies'. This was a skunk joint laced with crack rocks that snapped and hissed like campfire tinder.

◆◆◆

Jay and I raced from my restaurant to the Misty River Hotel basement.

Sitting on the dark, murky and damp carpet, the smell of bleach, piss and burnt tin foil was, and perhaps remains, the most excited I could feel. Having the food and a bottle of wine was key; it felt like an offering and didn't make us look like we were just scrounging for drugs, which, of course, was far more accurate.

Jay and I had become tied to the hotel. We would often wake up and go straight there, if we hadn't slept over, to join the regular scene. We were a couple of scruffy teenagers who sat in a smoky circle of half a dozen dead-eyed adults with skin like wet cardboard.

We were perched on the stale carpet, my view dragging to Jock, a bald and withered cockney who carried a startling similarity to Uncle Fester from *The Addams Family* – if the Addams family had been based in the roughest estate in Croydon and smoked bath salts. Jock was usually full of chat; chirpy and hard to shut up at times. But, tonight, something had him by the throat. His eyes rolled, pupils fighting for balance, and his body jerked and tussled in visible pain.

'Ahh, fuck me rotten!' he squealed, trying to drag on the spicy joint, as if the roach was barbed wire. His face winced, lips trembling, the paper crackling in protest.

From across the room, Ricky East started laughing, that snide, nasal snigger that always sounded like he'd just won a bet you didn't know you were in. He was another of the Misty's fixtures, a man who loved uppers, fighting and chatting absolute shit. Ricky was good-looking in that unfortunate way that older addicts sometimes are, the bones still handsome beneath the ruin. He looked a bit like Tom Cruise, if Cruise had done all his own stunts badly, just for the tramadol.

'Is it time then, Li'l Jock Strap?' said Ricky. 'Let's get it done shall we, princess? It's only gonna get worse!'

'No, no, stop it. I told you! I can't face it, bruv, not today!' Jock whined back, while pursing his lips to suckle the joint.

'It's painful to watch, mate. I'll tick you the goods for it,' chimed in Matt, kindly offering a pay-later scheme.

A look of defeat surged across Jock's face due to his inability to smoke. I clocked what was beating him. His tooth. He was in pain yesterday when I left at night and it had got worse. It was the most common physical rock in everyone's boot at the hotel, bar sobering up: rotting teeth. The insides of the mouths of everyone past the age of forty were horrific, with usually just three or four murky gnashers protruding, without symmetry, out of their lisping gobs.

Horno, a small little barrel of lard with greasy locks of hair hanging out of his bowler hat, was a kind but dim presence from south London, and was always praised by Matt as the force who convinced Elfie not to abort him.

'It's all right, Jocky. I'd take the tick, mate! Silver linings and all.'

Ironically, Horno seemed to have perfect teeth – on account that he actually had no teeth at all. Every weekend, I used to pack out my mum's quaint free house with an open-invite party; unsurprisingly, it almost always got out of hand. When she'd return, I could talk my way out of most of the traces of parties – empty bottles, rolled-up notes, broken plates. But the hardest one to explain myself out of was when she came home to Horno's dentures splayed on the kitchen table like a Halloween decoration.

'Okay, fackin 'ell. Okay!' Jock declared.

As he got up, I strategically lunged my hand toward his, claiming the spicy off him.

Jay chuckled at me when I did so, giving me a satirical sigh with a hint of real frustration.

Horno opened the drawer of the battered cabinet behind him and fetched out a pair of rusty pliers in a way that suggested this wasn't a rarity. It was as if there had been a spill and he was grabbing a drawer where the dustpan and brush lived.

They'd all done this before.

I supposed it was unsurprising; the thought of anyone here booking a decent dentist seemed as likely as a decent dentist booking a stay here.

Jock grabbed the stained pliers, along with a couple of grams of ketamine from Matt, and said the last thing I'd expected. 'Back in a jiff!'

I looked down the corridor, transfixed on Jock standing next to the mirror stand in the corridor.

Seeing him empty the baggy just under the mirror, I inhaled sharply on the spicy joint. The red ember spilled down the roll-up and then, crack, the sparkle lit up as I hit a rock. I held it in, slowly counted to five in my head and released. That sweet, metallic release. It was the exhale I'd been thinking of all day. That was the whole high, breathing it out and feeling the blood rush all over my being. It was better than climaxing, but felt even shorter and unquenchable.

Jay's hand immediately shot out to mine.

'Chuck it,' he cackled, as if he'd been wronged and I'd stolen something.

I quickly puffed again and threw him the joint.

Jay laughed as he tried to get a hold of the burning spliff, as if a hot potato had landed on his lap.

This all triggered an 'Oi!' from Matt.

My second 'Oi!' of the day.

'Do you want to know the oddest thing when pulling out dead teeth?' Rick leaned over and croaked to me as if reading trivia from a Christmas cracker.

'Umm, the oddest? Painful, I would imagine?' I guessed.

'No buggering shite!' cackled Horno.

'It's the blood,' Rick smirked, revealing the black of his mouth. 'The blood is a real shocker.'

I started to think of scenes that might ensue, and suddenly hoped he truly wasn't back in a jiffy.

'How much we talking?' Jay chimed in. 'Like *The Shining*?'

They all looked to each other as if in on something.

I could feel my face getting flush as I got more on edge from both the spicy and being kept in the dark. What the fuck was the joke here?

Images of Jock gushing blood out of his mouth like a demonic dragon started strobing my frontal cortex.

Why were they just smiling? Didn't we need an ambulance? Disinfectant? A fucking tissue?

'Relax, Al. There's no blood, mate,' Matt shouted over, in an attempt to relieve me.

Rick held up an 'o' with his thumb and finger and raised it to his mouth, whispering loudly through his putrid breath. 'Zero!'

Rick was right – that was bloody odd. It turned out that dead teeth don't bleed at all. They are dead, cut off from all supply, just hanging off your gums like a medieval decaying corpse off the Tower of London.

'SHITEEEEEE.'

Rattles came from the corridor, squeaky, breaking octaves in a harrowing shriek. There was a beat as Rick held up his crinkled can of K cider in admiration.

Jock stormed back in, bright red in the face and exhaling profusely with two nostrils caked in ketamine. He held up a little murky lump, marbled black and grey, that was once a tooth. The room applauded.

'Gimme that shit right now, lad,' he declared as he stormed over to take the joint off Jay, who offered no objections. Jock slumped down, grabbed one of my takeaway boxes from the restaurant and cracked open the crab linguine.

I couldn't believe my eyes. Was this not an emergency? Maybe dentists were all a bunch of crooks. How on God's earth was he hungry? Does the dead tooth just stay in the room with us now? My thoughts drifted to sous chef Dave, just hours ago ranting under his manly shrubbery of a beard about the crab linguine and the hours of prep, sweat, missed family and dedication it represented. He was right, of course, but I couldn't help wondering what he'd make of it all being devoured by Jock, under his rotten gums, with a side of 14 per cent cider and a joint stuffed with freebase coke.

I hoped I'd got all the shell out, at least. I suppose he was in much less danger of crunching a tooth now.

3

Junkie fried chicken

Serves / 4-6

Time / Prep advance
Brine - 3hours
Sous vide - 4hours
Cooling - 1 hour
Frying - 20 mins

Junkie Fried Chicken

1 Kg large Chicken thighs + Drumstick
- oil for deep fry

Dry Mix

500gr flour
100gr Corn Starch
2tbsp pepper - white + black (Fine)
1 tbsp Salt
1 tbsp Onion powder
1 tbsp Garlic powder
1 tbsp dried oregano
1/2 tbsp Paprika
1/2 tbsp Cumin
1/2 tbsp Cayenne pepper
1/2 tbsp Chilli - for a Spicy boy

Brine

1 litre ~~500ml~~ Whole milk
50gr Salt
1 tbsp Black pepper
Bay leaves
2tbsp sugar

Wet Mix

3 eggs
300ml full fat milk

☆ Brine - Whole milk/Sour cream/Buttermilk/Yoghurt
min 3/4 hours - overnight
☆ Sous vide - chick in gastro in Sealed bags
70c for 4 hours.
☆ Chick must be chilled before dunking!
Deep fry 170-175°

Culinary gentrification has hit Notting Hill harder in the last decade than a Metropolitan Police baton on Carnival Monday. It's true – and somewhat tragically significant. From the Banksy in the little bend at the top of Portobello Road, through the derelict arches of the Grove and up to the bustling Golborne Road, a change of authentic dining has been sweeping through.

Once a hub of family run restaurants and shops, its iconic Caribbean roots blossomed steadily through the borough after the Second World War as the Windrush generation landed. It's since been swiftly dominated by white public-school boys fresh out of culinary school serving fruity pizzettes, lemon tagliatelle and desserts drizzled with olive oil.

As an area that has always offered a contrast as the home to both the super-wealthy whites and the humbly working-class minorities, a culinary takeover was perhaps inevitable.

◆ ◆ ◆

As I entered my twenties, the punk scene in west London had moved well past safety-pins-through-lips, but it wasn't quite ready for oil-on-your-chocolate-mousse. It was, in truth, a totally flavourless stretch of time. It felt like the 1970s, 80s, 90s and even the 00s had possessed some defining showcase, some generational pulse of love, rage, prosperity, rebellion, shithousery, anything. But now the 2010s had finally ducked out for a fag break, drained of message and meaning. Rock 'n' roll was still very much dead and everyone finally got the memo. The pungent bubble gum that held bold flavours in past decades had been chewed stale. It was identity-less, a calm before the storm of change – and, looking back, perhaps that was its biggest beauty.

The Hound – a legendary reggae bar/nightclub in Notting Hill, a home to the Afro-Caribbean community for decades – was west London folklore. It was a shabby, dark, dingy cave-like space with sticky floors and its own stench that meant a lot to anyone who grew up locally, mainly due to its unbiased view on age. It felt lawless, and salivatingly exciting as a teenager. The most far-fetched variety of motley-crew customers who swarmed its cramped dance floor of a night made it feel uniquely unjudgemental. These were groups you'd never see out together in the real world. It was the only place on earth you'd find acne-ridden teenagers drinking, local Rastas blowing thick plumes of skunk, homeless people and then, also, Mick Jagger in the corner.

I'd love to say I left the previous restaurant because I'd out-grown it and was offered the big city job. As if. I was totally without a plan. Stints at restaurants would end when I'd have too much commitment, got too involved. A flashlight of 'this is life for ever now' – a terror of commitment – would take over usually around six months in and I'd just quit.

Life seesawed between the months I was 'in' and the months I was 'out'. When I was in, I could just about balance work with the chaos waiting for me off-shift. When I was out, the chaos swallowed everything; time became only a theory. No anchor. No burners. No structure. Just free space – and, for me, free space will fill with poison.

Either way it was exhausting. But the kitchen, for all its violence, was the safer of the two. Apron on. Burners lit. Somewhere to tire my hands out and stop them from wandering.

I came in to cook as The Hound was being taken over by Archie, a stern, robotic bloke in his late twenties with little experience in hospitality. He did, however, possess any entrepreneur's most valuable asset: unearned generational wealth.

To give credit where it is due, Archie was no fool. Although socially cold, he was driven, hyper-focused and, for the sake of good business, was unashamed to say things how they were. He solved Rubik's cubes disturbingly quickly and just for good sport: the kind of kid who either shoots straight A's at school or everything else in the building.

It was Archie's dream to have a cool spot, a social hub that you probably wouldn't imagine from a guy like him. The venue came with a valuable identity as a rustic iconic party den but, above all else, he wanted a food spot, a culinary feat, something that people would come solely for, instead of just rum, speed and a handsy dancefloor.

Taking over The Hound and bringing the kitchen up to a standard to cook safely was a gritty project by anyone's standards. There were holes the size of melons through the shed-like roof and rotting hunks of mystery meat placed in crevices; most notably, there was a manky single mattress by the rusty grills that the bouncer would sleep on after and, most probably, during his shift. I was hired in the kitchen for eight quid an hour alongside head chef Andy and fellow CDP Sammy, two other chefs who were around my age. CDP is the chef de partie, also referred to as a line chef – your basic middle-ground role in a kitchen, below sous and above commis. They were laid back and remarkably cooler than me. Andy in particular had a swag that's hard to embody in a kitchen while wearing chef whites. It was more than just a bandana and earrings; the total personification of nonchalant breeziness. They were also both mixed race, which bode well for the 'authenticity' of taking over a reggae spot, especially as all the original Rastas who'd called this home had been told they were no longer welcome. I'd previously been told that Sammy was someone who had worked and lived for this cuisine, having thrived at 'a bespoke Caribbean soul food joint' – a wildly colourful description for Nandos.

The menu was simple but clever, if not a tad culturally appropriated. Everything was designed to be served on your tray like a trendy school, or a Nordic prison. In your little sections of your tray, you chose your selection of fried chicken, chilli corn, green slaw, sweet potato, mac and cheese or triple-cooked fries.

It was a fast-food menu, but there was nothing fast about it. It was high-end 'cheat food', made from quality organic chicken thighs and breasts, brined and sous vided for hours before frying in a house blend of spices. That was the gimmick and it worked. It excited people and felt like an instant success. While it lasted.

The girl I was dating at the time struggled to handle dating someone who fried chicken. She was too beautiful, too outspoken and outrageously entitled – bratty, honestly, which was comedically attractive. She'd been seeing a lawyer and, in a move of questionable honour, left him to sleep with me – although, if we're being technical, I think both events happened on the same day.

Aside from rocky relationships, working at The Hound posed another unique hurdle: the kitchen hours. The dinner service would be a push, at times, but doable; the 3 a.m. rush, however, was a gamble. Yep, that's right. After the dinner period of a couple a dozen covers, there would be a five-hour dead gap for prep before the dancefloor would close up, prompting gaggles of wide-eyed, wonky-footed party-goers to head to the kitchen to get an order in before they got kicked out. Being in an efficient state at the rush was a test of cognitive ability that was totally – unfairly – out of my hands.

Now, Andy loved to smoke weed as did Sammy and I, but Andy was one of those cosmic smokers. You know them, the ones under the illusion that smoking weed isn't just getting high, but vital for a serene healthy life, like eating enough fibre or wiping your arse properly. To his credit, he functioned fine, mostly because he was always high; it was kind of like he never was. We would all drink rum punch in the dead gap and there lies the balancing act of still being able to make a chicken sandwich when the time came in the early hours rush. What my fellow chefs didn't know was the number of opioids I had been experimenting with at the time. I was either high or sick in a chemical malaise.

I'd got good at bullshit. I'd always spoken it, brokenly, but I'd become *really* fluent now. It was more than just bullshit. To put it generously, it was misdirection, covering up tracks, manipulating and real-life thespianism. I would often come in still tripping. And if I wasn't tripping, I'd be coming in off the back of a brutal bender that had started off with pints at the pub and ended with pipes at the hotel. I wasn't dependent on the junk. Of course I wasn't – like we all believed, anyway. You only know when you try to quit, which I had no intention of doing. I didn't solely use brown as a primary just to feel better again, or white for that matter. But what I did know was that I was becoming more of a passenger when I drank and used. The unknown – of where the night went from my first drink – was fucking liberating.

I would itch, sweat and seem totally vacant-minded, accompanied by occasional vomiting. On the whole, my grogginess and general tetchy nature was easily shrugged off as 'too much spliff', which was an acceptable excuse to the kitchen and easily bought, fried and eaten up by Andy and Sammy. However, there was an Italian turd in the fryer, by the name of Giuseppe.

Giuseppe was our KP. He was loud, un-PC and covered in the most meaningless and colourful tattoos. He loathed washing our shit and, in his free time, was training for his dream: to be a UFC fighter. He was also barely 5 feet tall and entertainingly easy to wind up. We would prod him, call him out on his conspiracies and question the meaning of his crass ink. My favourite was 'HATE' written on his right knuckles . . . and also on his left knuckles.

'There's no love from here, okay bro?' he'd explain defensively in his heavy Sicilian accent.

He was from a rough background in Italy and knew my pinned pupils and itchy skin was beyond weed. He would start to hint at what I'd been up to more and more as the months went by, like he had dirt on me. I would also come in with odd cuts, gashes and bruising from being in blackout. And, if that wasn't obvious enough, it was also common for Jay to just stumble into the kitchen, mid-shift, to ask something that definitely could wait. *'Are you off yet?' 'Do you have any baccy?' 'Lost my phone. Do you have the hotel's number?'* He was starting to dress like a roughed-up member of Babyshambles.

Giuseppe would smirk and loudly whisper to me, 'Owe money? You boys smoke garbage? I see you!' He'd point to his eye before releasing his totally tone-deaf cackle. It would get under my skin and he knew it. It grew unbearably irritating just knowing how happy it made him. Of course, I acted like I didn't know what he was chatting about, but it was hard. He worked out how to grate on me and it felt personal. Somehow, he saw through me and I was confusingly vulnerable. Most people see your bad bits and avoid confrontation at all cost. Even my girlfriend at the time was attracted to my shitty ways – or the first layer of it. There's an attraction to the guy with the cheeky grin smoking hash at the afterparty. But not so much the brown-toothed bloke smoking tin foil in the urinal. That we know now.

Tensions soon rose at The Hound. Many of us began to feel unappreciated, and couldn't shift the mindset; we were underpaid, uninspired and had grown bored of the menu. The dead space after what was becoming a deader dinner service became a laxer time to drink, as did joining the party when Archie wasn't patrolling. One night, as Sammy and I finished dinner service, we tucked into a bottle of rum from the bar. We drank as we prepped, but, more than usual, we were just being more open about drinking it.

'Bro, how about some chicken, eh bro?' Giuseppe turned to us, demanding.

'You're joking now, mate,' returned Sammy. 'You've eaten your weight in chips, brother. I'm not cooking anything more right now.'

'I want! Ali, you make me?' He pointed at me.

'No, I've gotta prep. And so do you.'

He was annoyed.

Seeing us laughing, it further irked his denial of more food; he wasn't hungry, it was a power play. This was an assertion of dominance, an invitation for someone to trigger him to show his masculine, Italian ultra-plume. He'd been accumulating being 'done' here for weeks. He was done with washing dishes, done with being in a cold country, done with orders, done with us. I was ready to bite.

Kitchens are easy to find work in, but hard to survive in. They're full of people who don't want to be there. And it's the same with front of house. Everyone's passing through – students needing rent, dreamers chasing authenticity, people who are too unemployable for anything else. Restaurants are society's purgatory: quick hire, quick pay, quick fire. And every one of them has a clock ticking inside – the moment where 'fuck this' takes over.

'Chicken, you rubbish asshole,' Giuseppe continued as his inner clock fizzled to the end of his fuse. 'Oh, you drink and take shit garbage in your face and little brain? Don't even have no respect for me?' He spoke in such broken English it was hard to totally grasp what he was getting at, particularly when he was fired up.

'You no even working here. You can't even remember last night, bro. You're a fucking wasteman, bro!' he continued in a stern rage while half chucking a chunk of ice from his sink in our direction, fishing for a reaction. One cube made contact, bouncing off my chest. It was followed by him sniggering with an unbearable sense of victory.

Fuck him.

I'd been stood there trying to harness my frayed emotions from severe chemical malaise even without a whiny Italian gnome aggressing me. In front of me, the stock was cooling, the sous vide was warming and prep shapes were laid out like sad geometry homework. My hands landed on a lime. Instinct took over. No thought. No morality. Just the pure kitchen impulse.

I hurled it across the kitchen.

It flew so clean, so elegant, that for a split second I didn't believe it had come from me. It was like I'd suddenly been possessed by Shane Warne, whipping a perfect citrus top spin.

THWACK.

The lime went straight into the back of Giuseppe's shaved head, bang in the middle of that shitty tattoo of Satan he'd got done in a backstreet studio for forty euros and a promise. That laughing devil face, all crooked teeth and bad linework, was taking a citrus uppercut.

Giuseppe froze.

He slowly turned.

The devil rotated out of view and was replaced by Giuseppe's actual face, all slack-jawed, Italian rage, like I'd just violated some ancient kitchen treaty.

A beat.

Then all hell broke loose.

He started grabbing and throwing anything with weight – sanitiser bottles, wet sponges, a whisk, a ladle, the full pot-wash arsenal – launched with the fury of a man defending his honour in a shit-smelling gladiator pit.

Thank Christ we kept the knives on the other side of the kitchen and that two stainless steel benches sat between us. Without those, it would have stopped being banter and turned into a very different kind of book.

'Madonna! *Vaffanculo!*' he chimed, under clenched teeth. It was the basic Italian every chef knows.

Sammy tried his absolute hardest to shout to calm it all down, but struggled to catch a breath from the hysterical laughter of seeing what must have looked like a Laurel and Hardy sketch.

I marched out of the back kitchen onto the front pass where we served the food and which was open to the restaurant. As I went by the fryers in full sight of the front-of-house staff and customers, Giuseppe came bounding from behind and pushed me. It wasn't so hard as to knock me over completely, but had enough purpose to get people's attention.

Sammy came straight up after us, the laughter now left behind. 'Chill, both of you!'

Giuseppe stared at me furiously, a bit of lime juice dripping from his ear, his two fists clenched under double hate tattoos. A couple of customers and waiters stared at us with eagle eyes to bear witness to the drama that was to unfold. Giuseppe declared his bombshell, the checkmate he'd been keeping in his apron for months.

He pointed to the fryer and announced, 'You should know! What is this man? You're all eating . . . junkie chicken!'

He strutted out of the serving area into the restaurant and straight out the front door, like a fun-sized Conor McGregor who had just clinched the featherweight title.

I was immensely flustered, panicked and, surprisingly, ashamed. Everyone was looking around – waiting staff and a couple of customers alike – expecting some response. I looked to Sammy for help, hoping for some allegiance, and perhaps understanding.

'It's not junk chicken everyone,' Sammy explained to a couple of half-interested gazers. 'It's totally organic and homemade with love.'

It was the first time I'd ever been called a junkie – or, at least, the first attempt at calling me one. It struck in that moment – the feeling of being outed and in a shaming way, even though no one understood it. I wouldn't wish it on anyone, neither human nor fowl.

Giuseppe came back in the next day and hugged me.

'I'm sorry, bro. Really sorry. I've just got to go. I'm just a tiger. I don't belong in here with chicken.'

He was such a funny little specimen. He felt so guilty for outing me in a fury like that, but he was clueless as no one actually understood a word he was saying. It's funny how I thought he was in his own world but he had this read on me that others didn't. Maybe they did and just didn't care.

I'm glad he quit. He didn't belong there – a small tiger trapped in the wrong coop. He belonged in a ring somewhere, sweaty and bloodied, fighting for something that made sense to him. I hope he's out there now, the fun-sized world champion of his own world.

◆ ◆ ◆

It wasn't long until Archie had a meltdown and shut down the kitchen side of the venue altogether. The numbers are hard when you're spending that much on produce just to be mostly battered and fried. And it was the classic case of acceptance, which is true of most venues, that drinks sales run the place. It was an end-of-night rum spot. So Archie fired us all, the whole kitchen, with no notice.

The very same week, that girl I was seeing reached her own melting point. At first, the lawyer-to-fried-chicken line was a joke. She'd laugh about it in bed, like it was some charming punchline to her little social experiment. But as the sex wore off, the humour did too. The line started to sound less like banter and more like a warning. It went from, '*Can you believe I've gone from a lawyer to fried chicken?*', with a rebellious giggle, to '*I CAN'T BELIEVE I'VE GONE FROM A LAWYER TO FRIED CHICKEN!*', squeaked through panicked realisation.

And, to be fair, she wasn't wrong. I was no catch; I lived at my mum's. I got her pregnant but could only half-afford the abortion . . . while still affording drugs. And I gave her head lice. Ultimately, though, it was the fried chicken she truly couldn't forgive and, with that, she dropped me faster than a portion of junkie chicken being thrown into the fryer.

4

Braised octopus with tomato, Chablis and a sweet miso purée

Braised Octopus, in Tomato + Chablis, Sweet Miso Purée

Serves 7-10

Cook 2 hrs

ingrediants

Prep
- 1 octopus, defrosted + beak removed

Sweat
- 1 fennel bulb
- 3 shallots
- 3 cloves garlic
- 1 tbsp tom puree
- 1/2 tsp pimenton
- bay leaf

Deglaze
- 1/3 bottle Chablis

Braise
- 2 tins tom/passata
- 2 tbs dark soya
- 1 tbs caper → + splash brine

Season
- Gastrique to finish
- Tarragon + lemon garnish

Puree

Blitz
- 2 large sweet potato - peeled + ~~diced~~ cubed
- 1 tsp Red miso
- 150gr ~~200ml~~ melted butter unsalted
- Salt to season
- Whole milk to loosen

Kitchen quiz time

Q: The nature of being a chef gives you . . .

a) Drive
b) Discipline
c) Social isolation
d) A mother off your back
e) A scalp flakier than parmesan on puff pastry
f) A rare anthropological insight into the fluid socio-cultural taboos of Western gastronomy.

Yes, any of them. Well done. Give yourself a star if you went 'f'. Make it a Michelin.

◆ ◆ ◆

Veal? I've been stared down like I've panko-fried someone's new-born. Venison? Glared at as though I personally executed Bambi's mother in the alley out back. Foie gras? It can clear the dining room faster than a table of five iPad-clutching toddlers and one passive nanny these days. By dessert, half the floor would be bracing for an impromptu sermon on culinary ethics.

I start to wonder if I should just serve ice cubes next and call it avant-garde, but that too is probably destined for hot water.

Culinary taboos come in waves – what's right and wrong. I'm not ashamed to say that I've tussled with meat. I was vegetarian for a year as a young chef, still cooking fillet mignon without tasting it, like a sort of blind, tortured artist. Then, one stoned Boxing Day, I ate too many sausages to grant myself yet another meaty mulligan.

But the majority of culinary protests are, for the most part, uninformed. Veal, for example, is a by-product of the dairy industry. If you drink cappuccinos or butter your toast, you've already voted for veal. Venison is crucial. I know it sounds like the kind of pompous excuse that a City boy dishes out at a Fulham dinner party to justify trophy-hunting weekends, but it really is important. See what happens when numbers aren't hit and overpopulation kicks in; it's horrendously sad for the land and the animals.

And foie gras . . . Well, yes, I'm still not sure what the taste could possibly be to justify such a cruel act of gavage. Foie gras must be fucking close though.

In recent years, however, a notable cut-off that I've felt customers get most squirmy about is the octopus. *What happened there?* There was the *My Octopus Teacher* documentary, about the man who wanted to trade his wife and son for a mollusc. Two hours of a hentai protagonist chasing sweet tentacle opened the eyes of millions to these eight-limbed wonders. The issue became fiercely political, with the creature now deemed by many 'too clever to eat'. I've fallen victim to strenuous lectures on regular occasions about octopuses and their intelligence. It's a bizarre uprising. There is no animal who longs for the slaughterhouse. Intelligent or not, all life wants to live. And if we were eating things based on intellect, I've literally worked alongside pigs that I'd trust to find ingredients faster than some human donkeys I've shared a kitchen with.

Perhaps that needs explaining.

After The Hound croaked, I went to cook on a farm's restaurant: Relish, in east London. Soph, the owner, was an old friend of mine and needed someone to take over the kitchen. Being young, dumb and in love, she bought a cafe-restaurant with her chef lover, Kenny. It was a cosy wooden shack-like spot on the river and within one of London's rare, fully stocked farms. It was a romantic idea – that was until he dumped her in full chef fashion for party, powders and loose girls. Soph was left clueless with a restaurant – and Kenny drank and used to an early grave.

In the kitchen was Anita, a no-nonsense Estonian, with the long, knuckly fingers that pastry connoisseurs usually have. She was in charge and, although cold, was remarkably work-efficient. She was also slowly preparing to leave, hence the new hands desperately needed.

Then there was Antonio, the Italian saving grace and a stern working family man with a crucial sense of at least a decent level of funny. Give me a tradesman who can show up on time and talk un-politically over a culinary 'artist' any day.

By the grills was Steve, an elderly cockney chef who would get out-waddled by a one-footed penguin. He had grown incapable of picking up the bins due to his back, but his keenness to still be in a kitchen was inspiring. He was the old culinary warhorse who'd reply, 'Yeah, all right,' in his East End croak to almost everything.

'How are you doing today, Chef?'

'Yeah, all right.'

'I need a side of endives with that schnitzel now.'

'Yeah, all right.'

'How did Antonio's mum's oyster taste last night?'

'Yeah, all right.'

Then there was Ginny, a stocky, outspoken sixteen-year-old who would come help out on weekends and after school. Being so young, the drive she had to cook in her free time was remarkable. She was just a child. But she was also a total cunt. I loathed her. She would refuse to help anyone else's section and she would cackle at anyone else's mistakes. Worse, she poked at Steve's frailness. I'm not sure what ties Soph had to her, but it must have been something deep, as I couldn't shake the little shit off.

Then there was Soph herself. She was so comically brilliant with a sort of rough sexiness about her. That was the 'look' growing up in our social circle: glam but punk, like the Spice Girl who nearly made it but shagged one too many Backstreet Boys – Feral Spice. She would toe the line of sexual forwardness so blatantly.

Soph was also a gracious godsend for me – and for many of our mates who just needed to do something, anything. Because I'd known Soph since a young teen, faces from our chaotic friend group would breeze through in brief stints to wait tables or scrub dishes. We were an abundance of the lost and directionless, and it was often a recipe for disaster. Gaz would help wait, but while doing so he snorted so much Xanax and ketamine that it would leak consistently from his nose and form huge streaks of encrusted powders along his forearms from him wiping his drippy nostrils all day. And the best part? At the end of the shift, he would scrape off the cemented arm residue to create another sizable line to sniff.

Jay would be on KP duties every now and again, but Soph tried her best to never put us together on shift after we cleared out every beer on site and ordered dealers to come meet us by the goat pen. There had even been a shift where she had discovered bent spoons, blackened from cooking cheap coke and bicarb on the hob. We were a dangerous combo, everyone knew that, and Soph loved to be a part of it too mostly – just not when she had a business at stake.

Lastly, there was Rose, the waitress. It would seem that I was destined to live every chef cliché going: the chef and the waitress. Rose was sweet, fierce and fresh off the council block. In all honesty, I was less smitten than I was petrified of her dominance and outspokenness – and, most of all, of getting her pregnant. That wasn't just because she had a boyfriend, but due to the fact she was so open about kids being her fast-track to benefits. It was hard to keep blood flowing below the belt when someone is framing sex as an HMRC strategy.

She'd hunt me down on fag breaks, and I her. She'd slip out from the dining room like a fox timing its raid, cornering me by the chicken pen. That's where we'd knot together – half-clothed, stinking of bleach and fryer oil, surrounded by feathers and fag ash. We both knew if it got out, it'd rub Soph the wrong way. And, of course, probably Rose's boyfriend too for that matter.

◆ ◆ ◆

At Relish, cooking around the animals was a kind of therapy. No problem in the world could survive a fag and a seat on the edge of the pig pen. Percy Pig, king of the den, ruled with stocky trotters, pacing between the trough and the hay where the other three piggies slouched. His three modes were sleeping, scoffing or shagging – often multiples at once. Shagging consumed Percy entirely. He'd squeal and oink like a tiny exhibitionist, mounting one of his ladies while Rose cheered, 'Yes! Go on, man-like Percy!' Absurd, yet oddly sexy.

Lunch service started sleepy – eggs benedict, scotch eggs, goujons – we eventually ripped up the menu and went full BBQ as summer loomed. Relish wasn't aiming for anything remotely Michelin; if you're not fine dining, you go primal. Big chunks of meat on fire summon the inner caveman, a predator devouring another beast. Testosterone-fuelled men respond first with the groin, then with pale ale and finally by shouting amateur marinade critiques at the nearest woman while inhaling smoke like it's a ritual.

Percy led his harem in miniature war dances, flames licked the low-hanging trees and I, spatula in hand, stepped up as the commander of this ridiculous, smoky apocalypse. Somewhere between this primal menu and chaos that couldn't be orchestrated, happiness existed – charred, sweaty and a unique gift of lost youth finding camaraderie: *Lord of the Flies* meets *Animal Farm*.

As warmer days crept in, the private dining aspect of Relish seemed like the big transformative step-up. Suddenly the sun set and it was decorated with upcycled fairy-lights, an open flame for a grill and a lengthy outside dining table. It was picturesque; the last glisten of the sun's rays scattered over the river as the flurry of livestock shifted into evening mode, making it a special hidden sanctuary. Private functions started to fill the evenings with bespoke menus.

One event was set down two large tables past the wooden stilts of the dining area, with the head of the table just at the end of the chicken coop. It was the first time I felt trusted to drive a menu and it was terrifying – although I didn't hesitate to take the opportunity. It was like orchestrating losing my virginity, but for twenty people. It almost didn't matter what happened; just being able to say I did it would have been enough.

The proteins? Slow-cooked octopus, lamb shoulder in a rich velvety Merlot reduction.

Most cooks offered an excessively fiddly way of cooking a shoulder: prodding it, inserting sprigs of hard herbs and splintered garlic like a failed surgeon. It was bollocks. With a quality cut, the only thing you needed was time.

'Reverse sear it, low and slow,' I said at the beginning of the shift. '130 for four to five hours and then wrap it tightly to sit for a further couple of hours, and let that sauce do the talking. Get the protein prepped.'

'Yeah, all right.'

At least Steve was listening, I thought.

'I'm not doing the remoulade,' whined Ginny. 'It's effort. I can just watch the lamb. Steve will fuck it up!'

God, I wanted to dunk her in lamb fat and feed her to Percy – the blind entitlement of her, and yet I still had a smidge of admiration. Antonio let off a sigh. He had worked in kitchens where Ginny would have been kicked to the kerb before service even started. Maybe we put up with her here because we knew her life outside the kitchen was rough. She was being bullied and lived in a broken home, and every now and again became vocally torn about it. She had her own walls forged from her own demons and, well, we got it in the end. I think all chefs got it.

'What's for starters, big boy?' Rose winked to me as she approached the pass.

I'd yet to decide whether her loud extrovertness was attractive or not; it was scary either way.

We knew full well nothing of sustenance would ever come from us. We were total aliens to each other: where we came from, our ambitions, her avoidable right-wing nationalism. We had nothing in common at all, really. She was open about the fact that I was the poshest thing she'd ever seen, so far as to say that she'd get laughed out the house by her family for bringing me home. Yet there was a connection, even in just a mates-who-snog way.

'Polpo,' I replied, knowing full well she wouldn't know.

'Yeah? And what the fuck is that, mate?'

'Octopus, innit,' I poorly flirted.

'Eww what? You're a dirty bastard, you know that, Chef?' Her grin was cheeky.

Mocking was Rosie's way of flirting. An East End thing maybe, but whatever it was, it was aggressively dominant, like some sort of shame kink: authoritative and with an erotic impact that unashamedly struck me.

'It's gonna go down all together, down in the middle, along with the pork and fennel sausages.'

'My fave, princess,' she finished before grabbing my crotch briefly but very firmly.

Borderline too firm, in fact.

This wasn't a new action to her punchline; it was a game she played all through the shift. How many times she could cup and grope a feel while no one was looking. She got off on it; we both did. It was silly, playing with getting caught. To be honest, it was a classic delusion that anyone might actually give a shit that we were secretly jerking each other off behind a pigsty.

For the menu, the heavy lifting – the long braises, the slow-cooked flavours – were done beforehand. The real show came when octopus tentacles and lamb shoulder hit the steel drum BBQ.

A time-clever menu, yes.

A chaotic spectacle, absolutely.

The drum itself was an ancient, temperamental beast, blackened and hissing, demanding attention.

Every now and again, I called for Steve, supposedly tending vegetables, and got back a flat, 'Yeah . . . all right.'

A pause.

A disaster.

By the time I arrived, he was lost in a choking plume of grey smoke, looking like a Dickensian chimney sweeper.

Guests arrived, wandering around the farm like they'd stumbled into some pastoral fever dream. Soph ran around like a whirlwind madam, directing, corralling and somehow charming everyone. Her energy was too much on paper, but perfectly tuned to this chaos.

Private events needed someone like her, a human lighthouse amidst the smoke, sizzling meat and rogue BBQ flames threatening to consume us all.

Somewhere between the charred lamb, oozing juices and the absurdity of grown adults fawning over the spectacle, the night became a kind of primal theatre.

'Service!' I chanted while I drizzled the charred tentacles with a dark-red reduction.

The smell was tantalising, a deep acidity of lemon, tomato and wine with hints of aniseed as the fennel barged through. The fragrant cacophony of flavour reflected my inner confidence as I lowered my face to the platter for final touches. It was the most remarkable feeling, the protein coming out exactly as intended, as well as the flavour and texture. The putrid stress that had been rotting in the pit of my stomach all day blossomed into pride.

Antonio placed the sausages on the pass and I the tentacles. Rose strutted over to take them.

'Aww, you fuckers. Poor piggy! What about Man-like-Percy? Could be his brother!' she protested while slyly brushing my groin yet again.

It wasn't the time.

I retracted just in time for Steve to put the scorched broccolini with tahini on the pass, and shoot me a questionable look.

'Yeah, all right?' he questioned with a sense of pride.

'All good, thanks, Chef,' I replied.

Starter platters down, I began to tear the lamb. The blade bone slipped out so satisfyingly it was almost erotic and I placed it rustically down on a bed of rosemary.

Just as mains were a go, there was a slowing of adrenaline, the peak of the mountain had passed and breathing returned. And there it was, walking towards me, to spoil my descent – a complaint, one of ethicality.

A tall, skinny mixed-race lady strutted over to the pass. She had dozens of silver loop piercings all down both ears and one through the septum of her nose, which weirdly was the first time I had seen that piercing not on a pig. She looked stunning, but also palpably politically opinionated.

'Excuse me. I just needed to say . . . Did you know? The octopus's brain is in its tentacles!' She blurted this at me like a pissed relative reading trivia from a Christmas cracker.

It threw me off.

I had nothing, just 'Yeah, all right,' triggering Steve to look at me in dreaded concern.

It was painstakingly entitled, a frustration that didn't hit straight away, but brewed achingly as the seconds passed, like one of Rose's firm crotch grabs.

What did that even mean? I thought while aggressively plating the lamb. What about those girthy sausages you were tucking into? Go look at the sheer amount of pig minge that consumed Man-like-Percy and tell me his brain was in his head. You could literally hear him right now squealing through the same piercing on your snout.

Those moments offered the clarity that customers should never interact with the kitchen. The entitled ignorance – watching me sweat my arse off while she strolled away like she'd just claimed the Nobel Green Prize – was nearly enough to make me stab my filleting knife into my own thigh. Or at least Ginny's.

Her attempts to mollusc-shame me didn't stick. The meal was a raging success. Every one of us in the kitchen was spent to the last drop of energy, muscles trembling, lungs screaming, fingers slick with fat and sauce.

But when it was finally over, the blonde beers from the end-of-shift iced bucket tasted different – and not just because they were knock-off Coronas. There was something in the exhaustion, in the shared triumph, in the smoke-stained air, that transformed them into pure Ambrosia. They were so good, in fact, that we carried them across the farm all night like spoils from a minor apocalypse, laughing, sloshing, swapping stories, the faint tang of BBQ and sweat clinging to everything like a badge of honour.

All the chaos distilled into blissful camaraderie.

◆ ◆ ◆

Relish eventually got sold. Soph gladly ditched the restaurant life, choosing instead a circus of touring musicians over grease and chaos. I never saw Rose again, although I like to imagine her drowning in a small army of kids, exactly as she planned. And Steve . . . well, wherever he is, I hope he's still kicking, and just . . . yeah, all right.

5

Wood pigeon salad with chanterelles and a walnut dressing

Wood Pigeon Salad, Chanterelles Walnut dressing

Serves 2 Time 30 mins

Fire roasted
- Pigeon Breast x2
- Rosemary
- Thyme
- Garlic, Crushed

} — Basting

- 100gr chanterelles
- tsp dried thyme/Sage
- Watercress
- toasted pine nuts
- handful of Pickled Blackberries — 250gr berries

{ 100gr Sherry Vinegar
3tbsp Sugar
Pepper corns
Star anise

1.) Bring to a Simmer
2.) Pour over berries in sealed jar
3.) use after 5 hours

Walnut Dressing

- 1tsp Dijon
- 1tsp honey
- 1/2 garlic clove
- 1tbsp walnut oil
- 1tbsp olive oil
- 1 lemon - Juice + Zest
- Salt + pepz

~ Mushrooms coloured over high heat with butter, thyme, Sage, garlic.

~ Season breasts at room temp - Breast side down, 2 mins per side until pink & tender.

~ Whisk Walnut dressing till fully emulsified

~ Assemble dellicatly - Pigeon just warm

1977, Paris

Maxim's is one of the holy cathedrals of old-world French dining, the sort of place that can turn a grown chef into a trembling boy – and vice versa, when invisible silhouettes were shaped into shining stars that change the industry. It began as an ice-cream parlour in the 1800s and, with enough butter and authenticity, mutated into one of Paris's most shameless temples of excess, a velvet-lined playground where foie gras shared a dining room with presidents, playboys, princesses and goose-stepping pricks of epic historical scales.

You can tell the calibre of a restaurant by the biodiversity of its clientele. The weak ones rely on tribes – all footballers, all actors, all hedge-fund hyenas on the sniff. Those places burn hot and die young. But Maxim's? Its regulars ranged from Edward VIII to Barbra Streisand, John Travolta, Brigitte Bardot and, for balance, Hermann fucking Göring.

In the late 1970s, Maxim's was peaking. There are eras in history in which it would be the stuff of dreams to be dropped: London in the 60s, Berlin in the 90s, LA in the 30s, the era of glam flicks. Paris strutted into the 80s with a shining demi-glace. Michelin was becoming the global yardstick of prestige and the

French were sharpening their Sabatier knives like priests prepping for mass.

Into this walked Nick – nineteen, baby-faced, English and therefore public enemy number one. Nothing boils a French brigade faster than a loud customer, except perhaps a British chef attempting their most prized trade. Nick was hungry, driven and had purpose, growing a skin thicker than that of a mallard as he persevered to learn the bold secrets of modern culinary greatness.

He'd followed the classic chef's pipeline – shit at school, scrubbing plates at sixteen – but was blessed with enough timing and lack of options to first land at The Savoy. That undoubtably made the Parisians tolerate him. He grafted, shone and, by the time he limped back to London at twenty-one, he was no longer a wide-eyed commis but a culinary weapon.

So came Hambleton Hall, a postcard-pretty manor in the English countryside, sat on verdant green lawn with an unknown future. A businessman with deep pockets and a vague clue had decided he was now in 'the restaurant game'. It's a common displaced affliction more present than spag and bol. I believe it stems from spending enough lunches drinking Château Latour in great restaurants, giving the illusion you know how to run one. Like all the hotspot slap-up business lunches have been field research.

Still, in that fever dream of linen and chequebooks lay the opportunity that would change everything. The owner, in a moment of hubris or brilliance, did what ambitious men do best. He gambled.

He handed the kitchen – the whole war-horsed, flaming grills – to young Nick. Sixteen to The Savoy, nineteen in Paris, twenty-one with the pass. The boy went from peeling carrots to steering the ship faster than most chefs climb to sauce.

From what I understand, there were very few chefs in the country of that calibre at the time. To say Hambleton Hall was a success is an understatement. It was a detonation. Nick rocked the very layering of the Blighty restaurant scene and became the youngest chef to gain a Michelin star outside of Paris. He was just twenty-three.

Celebrities, foodies and royalty flocked like pilgrims to witness the young prodigy. Prince Charles detoured his shooting weekend just to try to get a table. National treasure Delia Smith crowned it her favourite spot. And, most incredibly, the Roux brothers came to dine to see the fuss. For those not in the know, the Roux siblings were it: the godfathers of modern cuisine; the first to open a three-Michelin-star restaurant in Britain and the only one to hold it for forty years. And you can bet it was a shit-right-through-your-chefs-whites moment if they came to sit in your restaurant.

After the meal, Michel Roux didn't just ask to meet the chef. He summoned the *entire* restaurant staff – waiters, receptionists and teaspoon-polishing busboy alike – to raise a glass and declare: 'Nick Gill is the light of the future. The coming man of British restaurants.'

It was the kind of blessing chefs fantasise about while passed out on tomorrow's prep lists at their unheated one-bedroom shared flat.

Nick was on track to become one of the greatest celebrity chefs Britain would produce. He was a genuine culinary comet, blazing with purpose, leaving everyone else squinting and swearing in his wake. An unlikely malcontent child grafted to become a culinary genius and lived happily ever after. What a joy it would be to leave that here: that a star was born, struggled, but fought to shine without burning. That wouldn't be very chef-like.

Nick left Hambleton Hall and moved to London with his wife and two kids to start a new venture: Tall Orders on the Fulham Road, where tapas was served, in dim sum baskets, at an affordable £2.95. Patronised by Princess Diana, it opened to good reviews but was an unsustainable success.

As the 90s muscled in, the wheels came off. Nick's marriage collapsed. His wife retreated to the countryside; Nick, wanting to orbit his children, followed like a comet losing altitude. He opened one last restaurant out there. Critics loved it. The bank manager did not. He went under financially, then emotionally, then nose-dived. The man unravelled, thread by thread, service by service.

One night, drunk, defeated and unmoored, he turned up at his ex-wife's house demanding to see the kids. She said no. Nick – this culinary prodigy, a genius everyone had once crowned – became something else entirely, something feral. A fuse that had been hissing louder and louder had finally reached the powder. He forced his way in, beating the one person who didn't deserve an ounce of it: the mother of his children.

On the few times this moment is referred to in the media or by reminiscing adversaries, the truth of what happened that night is brushed over. The reality of the horrors of the violent outburst is underplayed, referenced as 'barging in' or one sudden hit in an act of madness before he came to his senses. It wasn't. It was an act of obscene brutality more life-changing than a Michelin star could manage. I won't get graphic, but a fatality was narrowly avoided, thanks to the intervention of their eleven-year-old son.

Nick turned himself in the next morning and received six months for wounding. It was a shamefully devastating moment beyond any rational conception and a rock bottom that would prove irreversible.

From what I understand – or try to comprehend of this abhorrent night – it was just that: inexcusable but shockingly out of character to anyone who knew Nick. And things were only to get worse. Prison would change him irrevocably, in a way the toughest of kitchens never could. He would allegedly cook for the prison guards and it made the rules flexible enough for him to do hard drugs. He near-fatally OD'd twice there.

As a final shot from reality, a further incident happened in prison. The inmates apparently grew furious at Nick cooking for the guards and, one morning, as he sat distracted for a moment, he was spiked with an unholy level of LSD in his drink, allegedly triggering a further re-routing of a stable grasp of consciousness.

◆ ◆ ◆

Nick had a brother – my dad – who had been a terrible drunk through all Nick's success and was in rehab after Nick's move from Hambleton, but who was now tasting success as a food writer. This remarkable change of scales between them was like two sides of a seesaw of talent and success: down to the pitted dirt before the see had sawed drastically.

Nick was begged and encouraged to get back to work by his admired chefs, but he would never work in a kitchen again. My family staged an unsuccessful intervention. It fell on the deaf ears of a once-great culinary genius.

The story concludes, or at least pauses, with Nick turning up at my dad's one day in 1998, where they had a talk that I believe was uncharacteristically and nostalgically warm considering his current climate. They spoke of being kids together and reminisced about different times, times I'm sure felt like a different life for Nick.

'I'm going to disappear,' he said. 'Please don't look for me.'

Nick was never seen again.

There was a lot of speculation about what happened to Nick; that he ended it all himself is the obvious one. Still being on the run with a different identity is another. My grandmother hired a private detective for a while. All we know is that no money was taken out of his account and his passport wasn't used.

One theory is irking to consider, but just before disappearing, he had apparently witnessed a murder and had to go in the witness box to testify against the killer. This opens a whole new strand of aching theories. What's for sure is that it makes you wonder what kind of crowd he'd been hanging out with to even be caught up in that.

I have periods where I obsess about the lost link in my complex family chain that is Nick, a paradox of a man about whom it was impossible to fully understand much when growing up – and is even harder to track down now. His culinary fire burnt at an awkward industrial crossroads, an era before celeb chefs when you could be a culinary meteor, then vanish before anyone could monetise the debris. Nearly thirty years later, no one knows what happened to him. Nothing was found; no funeral, no closure, nothing.

As a sober addict, Dad bought into the idea of a right to cash in your chips for a new life, even though missing his brother broke him on some profound level; that it's about faith and what you choose to believe, and that faith trumps truth when the truth is unbearable. He chose to believe Nick was in Paris somewhere, cooking eggs, living quietly, free and at peace. I loved the sentiment, yet when I think of my remarkable cousins, I can't help but think, he can't be. It would be too cruel if he were.

Recently, I spoke with both Hambleton Hall's head chef and Nick's old sous. Half-retired now, both men went on to cook for the greats and earn their own stars. Aaron arrived at Hambleton at sixteen, just after Nick earned his star. He told me he'd never worked for a force like him since, that his entire career existed because Nick lit the fuse.

For inspiration, I asked about his dishes. 'Turbot with leek purée and beurre blanc. Eel in chardonnay jelly. Passionfruit soufflé. And the wood pigeon salad.'

He paused. I thought it sounded like my kind of menu, if not slightly angled to please my gran.

'None of it sounds groundbreaking now, Chef – because *Nick was one of them chefs who broke it first.* He was doing that stuff before anyone else even knew it was possible.'

I loved the wood pigeon salad. It's very on-brand with my family – a love for deep game meat and a way to make a salad worth ordering.

Then came one last story. Aaron lowered his voice. 'Temper? Sure. They all had tempers back then. But we *wanted* to work for him. He wasn't cruel. Except . . . well. Once.'

I waited.

'The outside fridge. The one with the ventilator for all the live crayfish. He locked me in it.'

The sous howled with laughter in the background.

'Why?' I asked.

'It was funny.'

I snorted while I imagined the scene. It sounded medieval, akin to something involving iron masks and an armed priest. Then again, thinking about it, I once placed a low crate of live langoustines under a fellow chef who was snoozing at the tail end of a double shift having taken off his pungent Crocs. I felt worse for the langoustines.

It comes back to me more than I'd like – usually mid-service, with knife and flesh in hand, when I catch myself doing something well but wonder why it still feels like bugger all. Nick was twenty-three when the industry knelt before him. Twenty-three and already spoken about in hushed tones, already written into the future tense. At twenty-three, I was barely brushing my teeth. My victories felt microscopic: not getting fired, not getting arrested, not waking up somewhere with blood I couldn't account for, and cleaning out the fryers spotlessly. The gap between us yawns wider than a drunk's fly at last orders.

At twenty-three, Nick was handed a kitchen and trusted not to burn it down. I was being handed warnings. The same age, the same trade, but wildly differing trajectories, like two knives forged from the same steel but with very different cuts.

There's something uniquely damning about knowing exactly how hard it is to do what someone else made look inevitable. I know the hours. I know the graft. I know the toll. This makes it worse, not better. I don't get to dismiss him as lucky or mythical. I know what it costs – his drive and genius – and I know I never paid the toll when it mattered. Nick burnt straight through the atmosphere. I orbited, stalled, rerouted.

Sometimes I could stretch to console myself with context: different eras, different pressures, different demons maybe. But kitchens don't really give a fuck about context. They only respect input for output. At twenty-three, Nick was becoming inevitable. And yet, the uncomfortable part is I'm still here. Still cooking. Still standing at the pass. Still on the grills. When the noise drops and the work becomes muscle memory, my thoughts drift to him; not as competition – that ship sailed a decade ago – but as a measurement. He was the chef that I'm not, the greatness I didn't achieve, but, perhaps, the future I avoided. His brilliance that burnt so bright destructed before erasing itself altogether.

In the kitchen, there isn't a chef I think of more incessantly. He's a silhouette on my section, the star I chase without ever catching, the chef I admire whose food I never tasted, and the family I miss, without ever meeting.

6

Tagine à la Skippy

Serves 4-6 Time 15 prep 30 cook

Tagine a la Skippy

★ Tagine Flavoured Stew / West Agrican nut Soup

Veg - Pick + mix

1 Potato - maris piper / king Eddy
1 Sweet potato
1 large carrot
1 Aubergine

⇕

Veg sub in/out
½ Cauliglower
1 Courgette
½ pumpkin
½ Celeriac

} Peeled + Chopped

★ Blend along with Veggies > just garnish

1st Garnish

1 tbsp harissa paste
200gr Yogurt
1 lemon

Spices

2tsp Raz el hanout
1tsp ginger, peeled + minced
½tsp ground corriander
½tsp cumin
1tsp tom concentrate
1 tin tom/passata
400gr chick peas
300ml veg stock
pinch of saffron
5 cloves garlic

2nd Garnish

2tbsp Peanut butter
Soya sauce
2 limes

3rd ~~Garnish~~

Corriander
lemon zest
to finish
Toasted peanuts?

★ Roast half of veg to a char to add later for texture

What makes a good chef?

I'm not talking likes, views, infamy, the rugged sex appeal of acne-ridden, greased, flaky exteriors, or even cold cash. I mean, really, what are the core ingredients that turn a kitchen into a dream team?

I could be naive, but in most sectors, the answer is easier. Being a successful model is complicated, yes, but symmetry and malnourishment has to count for something. Being versed in times tables seems central to being a good accountant. And a total deluded sense of self-importance? Crucial for any sommelier. So what's the equivalent for culinary greatness?

I keep coming back to one line from Anthony Bourdain's *Kitchen Confidential* about who he wanted by the grills – a tradesman, not an artist. And it's true: the delusion only grows as the public marvels over chefs as celebrities. Everyone wants artists dribbling plankton foam over triple-poached beetroot, aerated through a nitrous oxide dispenser, posing gaunt and brokenly sexy like Jeremy Allen White. But the tradesmen? They're the ones who carry the kitchen while the artists 'gram it. I've worked with all the dreamers, the maniacs, the quiet grinders and the ones who make you question your own sanity. Most kitchens, though, are colonies of worker ants – tradesmen sweating in rhythm with the grills – while the 'artists' are out there, staged for a camera, sprinkling microgreens to tempeh like a woke Salt Bae.

A good chef? It's not glamour. It's persistence, pushing on through the smoke in your lungs and the burn marks on your forearms, having the obsession with relentless, monotonous perfection to do the exact same task impeccably, again and again with intention until your nerve endings are unbothered by fire. It's the tradesman's stubborn heartbeat at the centre of the chaos, keeping everything from collapsing into absurdity. The artists? They'll be on screen. The real work happens behind the flames. But all breeds have their merits, so let's see the contenders.

Coming in at 5 foot 6 and boasting a dense 80kg, hot off the boat from the slums of Bangladesh is Karim!

Karim was the fiercest thing I've ever seen by the grills. He had the most intense raised scars down and all around his face. This wasn't a one-time accident; not a drunken mishap or clumsy tumble. Thick, healed gashes framed every one of his facial features. It was a tell from someone who had survived hell.

He was some kind of specimen, one who bared an instant aura of not being down with the kind of risqué jokes abundant in kitchens. That was made clear from the get-go. He once shoved a commis chef in the walk-in fridge and slammed the door shut for being too slow to come out. The commis chef could have opened the door to come out instantly, but decided, quite rightly, he was safer in there for a few minutes.

Karim was so locked in, darting around the kitchen, swerving and ducking with precision that it was often hard to tell what section was actually his. When service got lost, you were glad he was on call. He was an ultimate team guy with an ideology that a fuck-up was on all of us, so he salvaged it from all angles like his life depended on it.

I worked with Karim at a Parisian-themed brasserie by the river. Lunch service could hit a hundred covers and, once the rhythm broke, the kitchen would hyper-focus, committing to the near-impossible task of staying afloat. One lost ticket or one stubborn soufflé and you prayed your strongest were on shift. Karim mesmerised me. Built differently, he was one of the best chefs in London in terms of sheer speed and focus – until one afternoon when I was on meat and he was on larder. He was finishing three salads at once, opened his refrigerated drawer, slammed it in frustration and barked:

'Chef! Chef! I need the herbs! The middle left!'

Our produce had just been delivered. The soft herbs were all lined up behind me.

'Yes? Which?' I asked.

'To the left! The left!'

I grabbed the mint on the end.

'No! No! More middle!'

'Which?'

'More middle!'

We played this bizarre herb-pointing game until I finally grabbed the right stem and laid it on his station.

'Nice, nice, yes. Thank you, Chef.'

Karim might have been the fiercest force in the kitchen, but he didn't know what dill was.

In fact he didn't know the depths of any dish he sent out. He just saw it being made and could recreate it perfectly with wrathful drive and stamina. This was his first kitchen job, part of a programme giving opportunities to those who'd endured horrendous disadvantages. Technically, he was actually just a commis chef, but he was a predator at the bottom of the chain. My first-draft pick for a dream kitchen? He'd be top of the list.

And next up, in the other corner, coming in at 6 foot 5 and just 85kg, the entitled, lanky bastard coming straight off the punt from Cambridge is Dev!

I used to work with Dev at Granger & Co., the Notting Hill hotspot serving yummy mummies who queued for hours to get baked eggs and to display their bright colours to David Beckham, often a fixture at the bar.

At best, Dev was a tardy, naturally lethargic but generally likeable chef. If you were on fire, he'd help put you out for sure, albeit with a frustrating lack of urgency. Maybe he'd squirt a fine stream of water from his 300ml squeezy bottle with sluggish aim, before refilling at great leisure. He had a poor sense of hygiene, was bad at cross-contamination and, worse, he would flatulate openly with remarkable confidence and invasive stench.

He went on to grasp pretty astounding success by cooking on social media, astounding for anyone who worked with him. Maybe I'm being unfair. He's creative with food – that's what he does and has earned a living from – across a range of cuisines. He has a real understanding of flavour and, with that, he makes menus that have put his name on the culinary map more than most. Still, I've never seen someone fuck up an omelette that consistently.

And in another corner, with hugely varying height and weight and very forgettable, is generic chef Bob! (The crowd that haven't left for a toilet break clap slowly.)

Bob is representative of a dozen chefs I've worked with who make up a considerable bulk of kitchens. You don't hear or read much about Bob because he/she/they are wildly uninteresting – just sturdy workers with limited options and a mild sense of apathy, meaning they'll stay put. Their greatest strength is not having any goals, so you can expect loyalty for years. Their biggest weakness is a general lack of personality.

And finally – falling from great height and bellyflopping into the centre ring – measuring 5 foot 11 and weighing 72kg of pure regret is chef Mark from the Plum Gate! The crowd *awws* nostalgically as he rises from a shallow puddle of vomit, wipes himself down and returns a tragic little wave.

Mark was a talented chef, with a tight work ethic. He was knowledgeable, experienced and creative with food in a borderline wacky way. He was also a fierce worker; I can guarantee there are plenty of chefs who would have thrown in the towel after awaking in a pool of vomit instead of getting up and wiping down. He was a great chef but, ultimately, a broken human: highly emotional, unpredictable, controlling, rageful and toxic (to himself mostly). It's a familiar pattern to many in the kitchen. He was run by fear – the most effective motivator by the grills, but the greatest catalyst to reach melting point. It's infectious in a kitchen and ultimately means his shelf life is never long anywhere.

Who comes out on top? They each have their assets, but boy is it a shit show in the wrong place. Dev getting out of a service cock-up? Karim having to come up with a new menu? Trying to get a fucking punchline out of Bob? Mark in charge of people? All disasters.

You come to learn in kitchens that the most important asset one can have is a desire to be there. It's that simple. There's nothing worse than sharing a section next to someone who is punishing themselves by cooking – something for a quick buck as they study the history of art or try to break big as a DJ, with an attitude that they're above all this. These are the ones who always try to go home early, who skim the bare minimum, who are painful to motivate and so glum that I'd rather share my station with one of Dev's densely aromatic farts.

What's interesting is the notorious association of bad mental health hand-in-hand with the intensity of the job itself. It is a fierce contributor. But what many don't think about is the kind of person entering the kitchen. Who would enter? Well, naturally, those with a bad understanding of money and labour – if they have any options in the first place that is. But, mostly, the kitchen naturally shelters the school failures, the unsocials, the obsessives, the runts, the odd ones; in short, life's square pegs. Although very different humans, that's what all the chef contenders above have in common. Karim had the roughest life imaginable and was beaten and tortured as a child with next-to-zero education; Dev was spoilt but had more STDs than GCSEs; and in what other sector could drunken Mark not only be accepted but actually put in charge of running?

The pairing of mental health and chefs has been forced into the public eye almost like a house-special cocktail in need of pushing. There's a romanticism to the gruelling labour and lack of HR, and mental health somehow got sellable. I'm convinced it's caused a lot of regular office-job workers to quit and join a kitchen in the name of rock 'n' roll, before realising it's not quite like they'd seen on Disney+.

I had a predisposition. Far before I set foot near the grills, life was spiralling. And, like many chefs, this was the only calling. I was unhireable in the most extreme sense – and that's where the kitchen will take you; offering an opportunity to just exist and possibly thrive in a way so many would never have the chance to in any other setting. The remedy can also turn to poison. It's no cure for the deeper stuff. It won't fill the endless hole, the ticking spiritual defect. Nope. That shit will ride you out no matter how much you try to grill, slice, flambé or drown, and when it's at boiling point, the hope isn't just for another chapter but a different story altogether.

Even stories that seem like a great culinary success often have tragic ends. Uncle Nick was the youngest chef to ever get a Michelin star outside of Paris, but I sometimes struggle to fathom his disappearance, never to be seen again. Nick's story was an anomaly growing up, one too painful for the Gills to really speak of. But it manifested itself in random acts of panic in the night, as Dad would call me and my sister to check where we were, fearing we had abandoned life altogether.

My dad loved hanging around with chefs. Not only was it his world, but it was a part of his connection to his brother. I once spontaneously went over to Dad's after an early day shift for a late lunch, where he introduced me to his friend Tony. There was something ominous about him. Most characters at Dad's were extravagant and loved to hold court. Not this one; he was quiet and reserved, but held a focused attentiveness through his engaging eye contact and grew warmer as the three of us sat for a late lunch to eat Dad's pork (he was always cooking pork, usually loin).

'Al's a chef,' Dad pointed out to Tony. He liked that I was. And I loved that more than anything.

I was sniffing so hard from a particularly savage few days – fuelled by cocaine by the grills and unknown houses – that Tony commented on my blocked nostrils. 'Sounds like a chef,' he smiled through a crooked alligator grin.

He actually wasn't reserved; he just wasn't a show-off, I realised. He was a unique character, totally his own kind of slick. It was hard to put my finger on it, but there was something palatable about him. I hadn't met a guy like him before. Was he a chef? I told him he looked too clean and well kept. He agreed. 'Less cooking these days.'

When asked what I'd been cooking, I began a rant about Moroccan tagine that ended up closer to goulash crossed with West African peanut soup. I had been cooking for dozens the night before; pork braised in miso and then pulled. But I was stunted by the veggie option – five porkless bowls. Without it, there was just something missing; shallow in depth from a lack of miso piggy fat. And so, just before serving, I finished it off with a dollop of peanut butter. They first scoffed at the irony of meat; that no regions that serve tagines eat pork. It was a good point. Dad gave me a look as if I'd said I rubbed it over my privates and entered the pig pen for Percy's feeding time.

'Revolting,' he said.

I pushed back. 'No, no, really, it works. Layer of nutty cream.'

His chef friend came in. 'What kind?'

'Oh, just goulash, but I put the base with Moroccan—'

'Of peanut butter?' he corrected me.

'Skippy, obviously, but crunchy,' I divulged, like some big trade secret. 'None of that split eco rubbish.'

'He's right. Well done, Chef. I need that palm oil in my peanut butter,' he agreed.

'If orangutans didn't die for it, it's no good,' I concluded.

We laughed, entertained more than anything by seeing Dad so wound up.

'You're just wrong, both of you,' he moaned to us, like a half-arsed headmaster. We chatted for hours: of goulash, peanuts, Japan, then the rest of Asia. I was dying to go to Japan especially; once, in the kitchen where I worked, all the chefs had a row over the best Italian spots, which ended with my head chef blurting out that the best Italian he ever had was in Tokyo. I couldn't believe it. Tony, though, concurred with insistence. Dad too.

'As a chef, I fell for it. You will too. Go.' I still haven't been.

I never saw Tony again. But I came to appreciate him in a different manner. As the years passed, I came to see him like most other people did: Anthony Bourdain, the soaring sharp-knife and blunt wordsmith of my industry. He was an unforgettable chef, regardless of status. I was in awe of the individual culinary swagger he embodied, while simultaneously seeming to be like just another chef. But he was a bespoke kind of kitchen force, a culinary giant to be reckoned with. His untimely leaving was a profound loss to all kitchens.

7

Fig and taleggio tart

Serves/8 Time/>1hour

Fig and Taleggio Tart,

+ Shallot Consit

Ingredients

3. { 5 square sheets Phyllo pastry
   { 100gr butter
1. { 2 Shallots
   { Red wine
   { 1 tbsp demerara
4. { 8 figs sliced/quartered
   { Taleggio
2. { 4 large eggs
   { 200ml double cream
5. { Thyme
   { Chives/mint/parsley

Serve with - Romesco,
Basil Sally V.
Pickled dill creme fraiche

1. Start with Shallot jam - Butter sweat, wine, Sugar and reduce till dark + Sticky
2. Combine eggs + cream. <u>Whisk</u> + <u>Season</u>
3. Layer phyllo in tart tin brushing with melted butter as you go. Slice hanging excess phyllo off sides.
4. Build tart - jam, egg, figs, taleggio and herbs.
5. <u>30 min</u> at <u>180°c</u>, Cool, Season

Behind a cook is a mecca, a place where the food, produce and attitude to service is meaningfully amplified – and, with that, a season to match. I cooked with a chef who would spend cash he didn't have just to be on the Amalfi coast when the lemons boomed. And my previous head chef would always grow melancholy around spring knowing he was missing snow crab season back where he trained on the Canadian coast.

The South of France is mine, just before September makes way. It's where I would try to flee to throughout large stretches of my teens and twenties. One summer in particular, I'd quit cooking and had nothing. I was discovering the danger of it. 'Expect poison from the standing water': William Blake never stood truer.

I was leaning in to that annual, bittersweet comedown of summer. Bitter because the warm, forgiving energy it hides you in was already slipping back into dusk. It's odd how that stress of 'back to school' season lingers long after dropping out. It was sweet as I spent the last two weeks in the South of France just outside Saint-Rémy for as long as I possibly could with whoever had room in the inn. I was clinging on like a rogue crustacean to a stray sea rock.

The seasonality of produce there is incomparable; the peaking of Mother Nature's greatest bits. The tomatoes are the best they will ever be anywhere for anyone, blushing in a full spectrum of shades. The flat-arsed white peaches are delicate and bashful, with tantalisingly quiet seduction and bursting with hidden exotica. Then there's the thick bulbous derrière extraordinaire of the yellow peach, sun-drunk, unapologetically ripe exhibitionists with sticky consequences staining linens and reputations. The au naturel fuzzy-haired peach – divine, soft and untrimmed – is an honest fruit, reliably available and understated. And let's not forget the immaculately hairless nectarines: slippery, athletically tight-skinned, smoothly engineered and often a generational preference.

As you may have guessed, it's not exactly a haven for getting laid.

Of course, there's the French queen – the sacred, one and only, regal fig. Its bulbous bottom bursts from the seam with sweet jammy goodness, pesting shoe soles and stone floors with its sticky ooze. Also, aubergines and courgettes are in abundance – something for everyone.

It's a paradise. Actually, I can't really tell how much I love it in France or how deeply I've come to loathe London. Perhaps I'd 'adore' being in a downtown Delhi slum wearing a mini skirt made out of rand more than what my existence has become in the toxic capital of Blighty.

◆ ◆ ◆

I was at my uncle's house, my mum's brother, that he rents to stay in annually. He is a great ally of mine, someone who always had open arms for me and without badgering me to tag along with his life. His kids – my cousins – became more like siblings early in life. I was in one of those blank slots of work. I wanted to stay here for as long as I could, in total denial of my lack of prospects. The amount of metaphorical dead space in front of me was endless; I was like a flurry of unrecyclable garbage flung into the Atlantic. I was avoiding, at all costs, the question: 'Now what?'

Within those few weeks, guests came and went, but I was able to remain as the constant. The one thing that sits in your back pocket as a chef is this ability to offer something for a bed to lay, like a leech that feeds as it feeds. I revel in scouting for French produce that adheres to seasonality far more than back home. Walking into a French butcher's, it's excitement laced with absolute fear. There's an aura the French emit that suggests a genuine irritation that you're here to buy something they're selling. The meat cuts are vastly different to back home, far more intricate and pernickety; they make a particular point of having a dozen different beef cuts, whereas many of our chunky butchers would happily just dub it all as chuck. There are turkey oysters in sizeable batches – as in, the preciously juicy oyster flesh on the back of turkeys. They push enough of these niche, round pieces of dark meat to have them just there on the counter in their dozens.

Dad was staying a few miles away on the outskirts of Saint Rémy. Every year we met in the town, him dressed as a mid-century dandy, me looking like a pungent dead-head. We caffeinated, I drank and we drove over to his party's house to spend the day together. We rolled into the stone pebble driveway and arrived to see my nine-year-old twin sister and brother, Edith and Isaac, and their big, bright-white, gap-toothed grins as they came bounding over to hug a leg each and squeeze endearingly. I admit I was slightly lost with them. They were young and I wasn't around much, and although I'm their brother, I still felt I'd ruin their family Christmas card. There was no confusion about whether I loved them, but I did wonder what

I was to them. I knew I didn't know the half of them, nor them the whole of me.

I waddled into the grand hall of this Provençal Downton Abbey with a sibling cackling on each leg. Their mother swooned in with purpose to greet me. She was anxious. Her greatest fear in life was feeling embarrassed and I represented a fairly polar opposite image to everything she was. We weren't enemies, but we just couldn't be further on the spectrum in terms of how we operated as humans. I think my existence represented everything that just drove her inner computer haywire: chaotic, unaccountable and, ultimately, just a bit feral. It was chalk versus cheese, shiny versus crusty, antibacterial wet wipe versus re-usable condom.

She greeted me with 'nice to see you' and 'how've you been?' as she slowly peeled her kiddos' clutches off my legs. Her eyes were darting to every corner of my anatomy; I could feel her anxious panic growing as she scanned my rough edges.

'You need to take a shower right now and put on one of your father's shirts.'

I remained mildly terrified of her.

I hadn't fought back against anything she'd said to or at me my entire life and I didn't intend to start then. It was not totally unfair – the fusion of Marlboro reds, cheap hash and buttery BO was amplified by this particular day's all-engulfing sun.

◆ ◆ ◆

It is always awkward to arrive at a lunch table alone, particularly with wet hair and without a guest. I slowly strutted over to the outside spot, flowers entwining in the canopy above. The scene overlooked a postcard image of Provençal country and the grand table was already full with a buffet spread and people. I approached like a stray whippet, still damp from a swampy swim, and I was greeted with tremendous warmth. Of course I was; in any other similar scenario, I'd feel totally out of place – not just in conversation but visually, like the festive turd in your nan's crystal flute of Bollinger.

But, when with Dad, I felt like an extension of the magnetising cool kid everyone wanted to be friends with. Dad was the person you wanted centre table at your dinner party; I've never met anyone resembling anything close to him. The awe and anxiety everyone felt to be liked or noticed by him was so palpable that it could even trickle down to the offspring when in his vicinity. It was incredibly calming, being under that wing; safe by association. I was suddenly Sweden in wartime, Harry Maguire at the Euros or just lucky ol' Ringo. Dad got away with murder because you'd laugh achingly – even ashamedly – no matter how personally inappropriate. You could find something funny or inappropriate, but not both. Profound wit was a part of his speech, just in the way someone might have a little lisp or an Irish accent.

At the head of the table sat an aristocratic widow who had clearly been the lady in charge for some time. She was older but not elderly, embodying a bold presence while carrying a warm eye to complement a playful grin. She looked straight to me as she patted the vacant seat to her right. It felt more nostalgic seeing her; I recalled I always sat next to her.

'Welcome back, dear Ali. Here's for you.'

She waved to one of the help who brought over a fresh two fingers of cognac along with a wicker basket, which she placed on the table by my side – between the fresh mozzarella and coppa ham, like it was any another dish. But it was a bread basket full of fag packets. There was real variety, too – from Lucky Strikes to Silk Cut. I didn't need to glance over to see how close to combustion my stepmother was getting. And I didn't care; I had pricey cognac, cured hams, the largest collection of smokes in Provence and Dad's allegiance on my side, for now.

As lunch ended, the savouries were cleared from the table, leaving crime-scene outlines of flaked pastry and splattered Dijon dressings, spotlighting where the platters had laid. All sun-worshipping trophy partners were excused back to the poolside, while the money-makers plugged their earpieces back in for cross-Atlantic meetings.

Dad jolted up and reappeared with a couple of the kind of weaved baskets you might expect from a Jane Austen scene. He tugged hard on my moppy hair and declared, 'Off we go, my boy.'

I grinned uncontrollably, almost embarrassingly so. It was just his keenness to stroll off with me; that it wasn't even worth waiting around for something effortlessly sweet, or an alcohol caffeine boost.

I pocketed a pack of Lucky's on the bold assumption they were complimentary and wandered off towards the distant fig orchard down the dusty, barren hill with Dad and Edith, while Beetle – Isaac's nickname – trailed at my feet.

It was a funny new chapter, being aged nine, as the twins were; it's an age when adults begin to engage in more profound conversations with you. Nine-year-olds can remain totally naive to their surroundings, still playing wholeheartedly in their own little fictitious world, yet they have moments of grasping the trudges of life in the real world. Sometimes I felt Edith and Isaac were beginning to feel sorry for me; often, as they looked at me, it felt like they worried. Sometimes I thought they were just little shits.

I wasn't sure what a good place looked like, but I wasn't in it. In life, I mean; that French estate fit just fine. I thought I'd seen it in others. It was alien. I'd been in better places, but they also were kind of shit; they just felt better comparatively. This was a year when I'd particularly felt the one-way dumbwaiter. It was confusing. Everyone seemed to be gaining momentum with purpose, so why was my trajectory so aggressively downwards? There was some blueprint to life that I didn't quite get. The prerogative of no prospects and getting aggressively high was camouflaged by youth; a fucked-up teenager wasn't breaking news, more a rite of passage than cause for concern. But, at twenty-three, the years were ageing my slick camouflage gear into a nauseatingly fluorescent high-vis onesie.

The twins climbed fearlessly in an attempt to grab the figs perched at the top, beaming in the dry rays of peak summer French sun – Edith for no reason other than the fruit being hard to reach, while Isaac shakily followed, simply because Edith was smiling.

I could feel Dad looking at me as we began to pick the purple figs, so full that the tearing skin could hardly hold their thick-seeded flesh.

'You all right, Al?' he asked with a slight change of tone.

'Yeah, fine. Bit hot.'

'Back in London, how is life? Any cheffing when you're back?'

'Yep, yep. I'll get something.'

He chuckled and dubbed me 'Kevin the teenager', as he always did when I replied unenthused, then pointed to my ribs where a light red rash had been forming.

'Your psoriasis is coming along nicely,' he prodded.

I hissed back, while trying not to give him the satisfaction of laughing too heavily.

'It's your crappy genes, you know that? How do you get rid of it?'

He smiled. 'Some creams help sometimes, or a dip in the Dead Sea. It sorted mine for a bit, but you don't really.'

Vaseline and the West Bank didn't feel like useful tips in the slightest.

'Anxiety and drugs, that's what that really is,' he said, picking from the tree with nonchalance.

I opened up a particularly bulbous fig, pressed my thumbs into its bellied centre, tearing the skin and exposing the seedy, thick, burgundy insides. I bit, tasting the perfectly sweet fig, before jamming the entire figgy tennis ball into my mouth and shrugging at him. He laughed at my lack of reply and avoidance.

As I said, nine is a defining age where words acquire gravity for kids and will snap them out of their little fantasy world to nose around when they should be on standby mode.

'Drugs, Daddy?' loomed a voice from up in the trees.

You don't hear that often. Not this far outside a Soho House cubicle.

'Yes, children,' Dad replied, with satirical aloof, before adding, 'Dad's three rules?'

Edith replied like a little teacher's pet looking for marks. 'No tattoos, no motorbikes and don't be a heroine.'

'Close, Edith!' he replied. 'Try not to break all three like your big brother.'

Beetle chimed in. 'He doesn't even have a motorbike.'

He began to giggle, not fully understanding the full comical value of his implications.

Seconds passed before his little schoolboy giggle jolted us all into a slow burst of hysterics, Dad's deeper baritone cackle leading the two high-pitch giggles coming from the tree tops. It was signature Gill humour; tragic hilarity, and criminal not to embrace howlingly.

Back then, in general life, the luxury of contentment felt a totally alien concept. I was wired for discomfort and to overdose on anything that took me out of it. Right there, in that orchard, it was a rare moment in time, eased from obsession. I had no desire to be anywhere else in the world, nowhere at all but under the large, wavy fig leaves with my family.

As the hours passed, the sun dropped, but the heat just sat there, directionless, as if it wasn't even sourced from the sun any more and was just hanging in the very air itself. We began to stroll, with sticky soles, out of the fig orchard, with overflowing wicker baskets and achingly worn grins.

As we walked back to the house, I shared a rare heart-to-heart with my old man. Things weren't okay, not even close, but he was always great at calming me on what felt like unique problems, as if he'd had them all before: a lack of momentum, people, life. 'Don't let it stop you from being happy,' he said. When I was a child, he had this calming ability to turn anxious impending doom into a smile. I would be tearily panicking over unfinished homework, which he remedied by eating it, allowing me to use the classic excuse of 'my dad ate my homework'. He was good at projecting that things were really, almost always, okay.

I wish I could remember more from this walk, though I can still feel the warmth when I hover above its memory. But I think the ending dominates the stage, blocking out the substance – and, worst of all, something as precious as a hug between father and son. I held him and, as I squeezed, he flinched suddenly, like a spaniel having his tail stepped on.

'What?'

'Oh, it's nothing.'

How wrong he was. This moment would stay with me most vividly – a golden hour holding a basket full of figs, the very last memory with my dad while under the illusion that everything was going to be okay.

8

Truffled egg toast

Truffled Egg Toast

Ingredients

3cm-thick slice of square white bread
150gr fontina cheese
2 free range eggs yolks
1 tsp truffle oil
Salt + peps

- lightly toast bread, cut shallow square hole in centre
- Scatter grated fontina evenly around slice and pour yolks in welled centre
- Oven at 180°C for 3mins - Melted cheese - Runny yolk
- Finish with truffle oil

1 serving

10 mins

There is a spot on the corner of Brewer and Rupert Streets in the heart of Soho, a purposefully blackened bar that I used to work at: Spuntino. It's a corner that has always been considerably sketchier than the rest of Soho. It's sandwiched between four hand-job parlours, a couple of homoerotic leather diaper shops, multiple dealers loitering at nearly every angle and a pavement scattered with circling crackheads, like seagulls over a battered chunk of cod. If Boy George was a city planner, his job would have started and most probably ended on this little corner of Rupert Street.

Spuntino was a hidden gem created by the late, great Russell Norman. For those not in the know, Russell was the young rock star of hospitality. He was remarkably good-looking for a restaurateur, oozing charisma and energy in such a way that you could tell there was magnetic trouble to him. His restaurants were Polpo and Polpetta, but his real love, his baby, was the late-night speakeasy-themed spot, Spuntino.

Returning from France, I landed a job bartending here. I would occasionally switch between bar and grill because of sanity, I suppose; I was profoundly lonely and a change to working in front of house seemed attractive. I was broke, earning about a fiver an hour, but working here, at least, I didn't have to pay for booze, which upped my net pay significantly. The set-up for Spuntino was one large square bar that held around twenty bar stools facing two bartenders. It was like a stage – and the most on show I'd ever felt at a job.

Downstairs was the kitchen. The menu was like it had been designed by a stoned teenager who'd been asked what his last meal would be: brisket sliders, lobster mac 'n' cheese, tempura brioche burgers and the infamous truffled-egg toast. The latter was so overwhelmingly present in the room when someone ordered it; getting hit by the truffle oil that was clouding off the steaming cheese was unavoidably invasive to all the senses. It became the iconic dish of the venue.

Days at Spuntino were mostly spent drinking the tap ale as it was hard for management to tell a loss from tap, while gazing out the window people-watching: spotting which lampposts and bollards the dealers would hide their drugs in; seeing just how mad the mind is capable of delving as the shoeless moaned at tourists; and watching the middle-aged blokes wearing low-angled baseball caps stroll down the alley to suddenly swerve a right angle into Li Li's Blossoming Lotus massage parlour. It was golden daytime TV, like watching all the origin stories to a Jeremy Kyle show in real time, and often it became immersive. Crackheads, sex workers and just the plain old mentals would dart into the restaurant, screaming profanities, stealing pictures with no real prerogative, and, most often, nicking spoons laid out on the bar – with zero fightback from me.

There was a new meaning to shitting where you eat that I would not recommend. After shifts – drunk and out of powders – I'd get high with some of the crackheads and share their black-clouded pipe when locking up drunk and alone. The next day, one of them came in to steal the cutlery. My manager half-attempted to chase him out, but the crackhead stopped to fist-bump me on the way out with a ''Ello, my man!', sending my mind to recall the charry pipe I shared with him last night, triggering my manager to look at me in deep concern, and for my bollocks to climb straight up my throat.

'Crazy bloody fuckers. Get out, stay out.' It was a poor attempt by me to brush off the scent – and after he had left and couldn't hear me, of course.

It was one of those small moments, but a big picture-painting of just how far I'd slid – a moral descent that didn't really sting any more. Past the initial jolt of remembering a blackout, I just didn't really care. When I think back to the panic of Giuseppe outing me as a junkie at The Hound, that felt almost civilised in comparison. This would have looked far odder and I think my blazingly unbothered nature is what threw off my manager from reading more into it.

It was a show of acceptance of – or, at least, apathy towards – the skin I was in. Shame grows flavourless eventually and embarrassment was no longer so palatably bitter. After a while, it loses its sharp taste, it stops burning on the tongue and fades to background noise, like the low hum of the fridge or the unanswered oven alarm. You get used to it. It's something that's just part of your uniform now, like the burns, the cuts and the stink of fried fat in your hair.

Like all of Soho, night is where Spuntino became its true self. The bar drew full from 7 p.m. on the dot, opening with the smell of rich acidic beef and deep-fried panko that warmed the air, which occasionally would get trumped by the cheesy truffle coming out on top when ordered. It was food that excited everyone. I never worked in a restaurant so in demand. People craved it. It was a guilty pleasure merged into an eating-out experience. I would help the chefs with prep in the kitchen, but on the whole I didn't feel envy for not being in there more, mainly because the floor was so distractingly stimulating. Past dawn, it turned into one of the loosest bars I've been in.

The clock would strike 10 p.m. and the bar would slowly morph into an intimate, lawless party. Everyone faced one another, with us bartenders bang centre stage. It was like everyone knew one another every night, even with a completely different batch of strangers. Customers would insist on buying shots for everyone, cocaine was accepted regularly and being a bartender seemed to serve as an aphrodisiac. I've never experienced it again in my life and I can assure you it was an unearned benefit afforded to Spuntino bartenders by default. Girls, boys and everything in between would flock to Spuntino by the dozen, looking to jump the first thing they saw. The clever old design of the place meant that the first thing they saw was us. Partygoers of all shapes, loud or reserved, and from all walks of life would shove numbers in our pockets while darting tongues down throats, and even staying on for clean-downs.

The streets outside sweated rich and poor, beggars and spenders, piss and perfume. The furry two-man bicycle taxis, blaring Katy Perry and offensive to nearly every sense, prowled for naive tourists like neon sharks. Everyone was either chasing, running or convincing themselves otherwise. Inside Spuntino, the air got thicker by the hour – not just with fried panko, beef fat and truffle oil trying to cosplay sophistication, but with human hunger. The place became a little pressure cooker of lust and loneliness, champagne desires and pale-ale budgets. You'd see people arrive polished and upright at seven, and by midnight they'd be leaning over the bar like they were confessing their sins to a priest: pupils wide, words slurred, hands lingering too long on glasses they didn't pay for. They were mostly looking for someone to talk to – and we gave permission to be feral, to let off, to forget, to wake up tomorrow and know there's nothing to feel apologetic for. Well, not at my end, anyway.

One day, as I took a bottle of spirit out of the bottle rack, I spotted my battered Nokia laying there. I would lose my phone constantly and thus was notoriously hard to get hold of, which had become an ongoing moan from all friends and family. I fetched it from the sticky metal shelf and held down the 'on' button. It began buzzing. And buzzing. And buzzing. Buzzing with texts. Buzzing with missed calls. Buzz. BUZZ.

It felt cinematic, like in the movies when some tragic news is being delivered. I could hear the blood rush to my face as this little phone continued. Buzz. Buzz. BUZZ. This shitty 90s Nokia was buzzing my distant being back into reality.

The messages came, one after the other. From Dad: 'Al? Where are you?' and 'Call me'; one from Flora, my sister: 'At Charing Cross. See you there?'

I was in a total freefall.

Dad had flinched from that hug in France the previous month because of tumours all up his spine. Hopes were not high, but not totally dire. He was due an operation and I said I'd be there, I think. I could hardly remember what day it was, even now. Everything suddenly felt nauseatingly blurry.

I dropped the gin and ran out of Spuntino's mid-shift – no goodbyes, and for the last time – to go straight to Charing Cross Hospital. I entered A&E.

'I need to get to E wing, the cancer ward?' I stuttered to the lady behind the glass.

'This is A&E, sir,' she began and finished, assuming that cleared up everything.

This is the hospital? Aren't all hospitals A&E? My only hospital experience up until this point had been in A&E, almost exclusively from blacking out. She was more empathetic on seeing my hopelessly confused face.

'You need to go through the on-street gated entrance where you'll come to large lifts that can take you up to the ward.' She smiled, semi-forcefully. I began backing off while thanking her.

I went out into the street while trying to decipher directions from Flora. As it turned out, hospitals are fucking mazes. I walked through the army of robed smokers, some still holding fluids, past the large doors and into the unexpectedly huge space.

It was gloomy: the lighting, the apocalyptic, limping people and, most strangely, a flurry of shops and cafes like a mall. It was what I imagined the stomach of a senior cruise ship to feel like. I'd just been with Dad a couple of days ago, but in another hospital, when he sat and did his chemo and it felt brighter than all this. There had been an odd sense of happiness in the community getting chemo, a camaraderie of laughing with one another. Plus, he'd been so immaculately dressed, as always, and taking the therapy with such nonchalance that it felt like a less serious occasion when he was wearing a three-piece purple tweed suit with a cravat.

I came out onto the ward and was buzzed into the clinical hallway by two girthy nurses. It was different here; this was new territory and had an instantly more sombre feel than the chemo circle.

'Hi, can you help? Gill, please, my dad. He's here.'

She looked at her clipboard briefly before pointing me to the first door to the right. It said his name on the whiteboard and I wasted no time going in. I took one step into the room.

'Hi, Al.'

He smiled at me faintly, lying there on the hospital bed, tubes in his nose and face the colour of old parchment. There was no bright tweed suit, no glint in his eye – just a thin hospital gown and Flora sitting beside him, smiling the brittle smile of someone who was already grieving.

I tried to say something – anything – but nothing came. My mouth opened, frozen. My whole body locked. He looked so small, so fragile. I hadn't truly grasped anything until now.

I stepped back, then out of the room entirely. Something began to break loose inside me, a kind of eruption. I stumbled into the disabled toilet and collapsed onto the cold tiles. It felt like my bones had melted. Something was coming, but there was no clue what. It could have been projectile vomit or the precursory moments before fully shitting my pants. But no. It was tears. They streamed out of my silent, bright-red face. I hadn't cried properly in years, not since I was a kid when I used to cry a lot, and I loathed with fury how easily the tears came.

Somewhere along the way, the pendulum swung and I turned to stone. Now, all those stored-up tears were flooding out. I was choking on them – gasping, blind, shaking. My legs were useless. I was in a freefall and now everything in me was about to hit the concrete floor.

For weeks, I'd refused to see it, numbed it, pushed it away. But seeing him like that, pale and breathless, tubes and wires where laughter used to be, there was no more denying it.

Dad was dying.

A nurse helped me to my feet. He was covered in tattoos with those huge holes in his ear lobes – the un-nursiest nurse possible. He looked like a football thug in fancy dress for Halloween. I later learned he was a musician and was terribly unfulfilled, so he gave it up for something meaningful. He helped clean me up and carried me as I leaned my full weight on him, holding me with real care. It was new – another bloke helping, even when he saw me cry. I was half-expecting to be mocked, but, no, he gave a shit. And I could feel it, which left me even more speechless.

I was suddenly terrified of time. I needed to see my dad.

I walked back into the room – puffy-faced, blocked nose – thinking I could get away with no one knowing what had just happened.

'Had a little moment?' he smiled to me.

'A little moment'; that was one way to put it. He had always been blessed with a calming way with words.

I sat next to him and held his hand while desperately attempting to keep my watery eyes from breaking.

'I can smell the truffle,' he added. The oil from the truffle egg toast was in the fibre of my being.

'Well, you tell him what happened last night,' he said to my sister.

She was my full older sibling; we were close-ish – similar in parts, opposites in others. She was head girl and an Oxford graduate, but enjoyed crude humour. Our similarities were easy to dissect. She and Dad had this connection that I wasn't part of; it had always been that way. They always teamed up and were in on things, like a club. I was the odd one out.

'Shat himself,' she smirked.

'Right through,' he nodded.

We laughed, all together. It was what we did best in times when we shouldn't.

Afternoon moved into night in what felt like seconds. The nurses came round to say visiting time was over. It made me nearly sick hearing it.

Time to go? Where?

I refused their request, ready to fight them profusely for enforcing the rules. But they just nodded; there was no fight-back. That felt worse in a way. It was an understanding that the rules were out the window in a place like this, in a situation like ours. It opened Flora's eyes to it, too. She would be back soon enough and we'd tag each other in and out.

Nights went by and Dad's cognitive state went a bit airy. He was never really gloomy. It was like he had full acceptance that he was completely out of control. They eventually gave me a blow-up mattress on which to sleep beside him. Nights were close to sleepless.

My skin was always bad. Most chefs battled with flaky, rashy skin, as we were constantly in a job immersed in bacteria and stress. But now my blood was staining the blow-up bed's beige exterior as my psoriasis had got so bad my arms and face were just open wounds, bleeding by themselves with no reason, itching on the cold floor while enduring moans throughout the night from patients in semi-conscious horrors.

The only time I left Dad's side was when an AA meeting came up to his room and I had to go pick up from my dealer down at A&E. He knew I would, and just said, 'Don't smell when you come back.'

Food was sent from Michelin chefs as admiration. What do you send a sick food critic? Well, I'm sure some would send Milanese, with a side of anthrax, if they could. But many sent their bundles; his taste was leaving, so heavy flavours – extra-spicy or hard-hitting. He was able to react to the smell of truffles, even though he seemed to be in an unconscious state.

Visitors came and went, as we both deteriorated. But I wouldn't steal his thunder this time.

My stepmother would dash in occasionally, completely lost in what to do. My heart changed for her in these moments; she was losing her person, my nine-year-old twin siblings in each hand, eyes darting around the ward, unable to fully process the gravity of what was looming.

We had one night when it felt noticeably quiet on the ward. It was briefly calming. The room was so high up that it had a remarkable view of London. At night, the motions of the rides from Winter Wonderland in Hyde Park swayed in the distance. I laid behind his bed and we talked. He had started to pull out a needled tube attached to his nose in his sleep and I was trying to stay eagle-eyed to keep his hands away from it.

'You'll watch over me while I sleep, Al?' he asked endearingly.

'Always, Dad,' I replied, gulping back any further emotion from surfacing.

He went on to tell me how funny it was, how life worked out, how the roles had reversed.

I didn't see it – the funny, nor the life working out bit.

'What do you mean?' I prodded.

He drifted a little, his words coming slow and slurred with exhaustion.

'The most scared I ever was,' he said, 'was watching you sleep as a baby. I'd stay up for hours, just staring, counting each breath, terrified I'd miss one. I could hardly look after myself and, suddenly, there I was, responsible for this tiny thing.'

I wasn't built for this. My chest felt like it was splitting open. Tears spilled freely now, hot on my face as I lay beside him – my throat locked raw in agony, fighting the sobs clawing to get out.

'My boy will keep an eye on me,' he whispered.

I held his arm until he slept and I continued to weep silently through the night. I kept my eye on him, in turns with my sister, until he stopped breathing altogether.

It was a clever dish, the truffled egg toast. Simple, memorable, tainted. On 10 December, I try not to think of it.

I think of the figs.

9

Ketty tuna (Eastern niçoise salad)

Eastern Niçoise

Serves 2-4

Time 35 mins

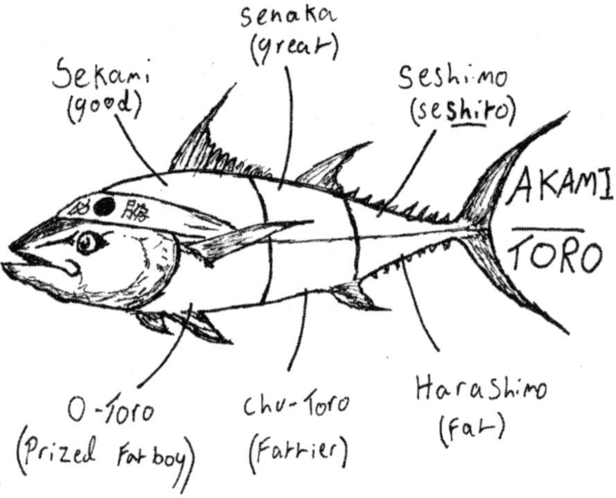

Tuna - 400gr loin

Neutral oil for Searing

Potato

1 tsp togarashi

1 tsp Seasame seeds

nori flakes / crushed dried seaweed?

150gr New potato

Salad

100gr samphire - lightly blanched

Cherry toms

pickled cucumber - through mando

Radishes

Salad leaves - Frizze + Shisho

2 ~~poached~~ soft boiled eggs

Avo - for puree - blend with seasame + Yuzu

black seasame for finish

Yuzu dressing

2 anchovy fillets - minced

1/2 garlic clove - minced

1 lime

2 tbsp Yuzu

1/2 tsp wasabi

~~2~~ 1 tsp honey

1 tsp mirin

2 tbsp light soya sauce

1 tsp sensame oil

Chilli flakes

There was no sell-out dish, no plate, no animal that yearned for the catch, nothing more universally appealing to the customer than tuna. It was a menu's safety net, the culinary comfort blanket, a beast that was guaranteed a reception and the crowd-pleaser that transcended class, budget and taste. Students could order it to feel prestigious; billionaires could order it out of lack of interest. It reliably raised pencilled-in eyebrows and loosened Gucci wallets globally, all thanks to the Japanese. It was a timeless classic. Well, sort of.

Like any culinary hero, tuna's arc was notable. In early Japan, it was far from aspirational, noble or remotely prestigious. It was trash, a problem meat, a fatty flesh that spoiled quickly in warm climates – and thus good for feeding in-laws and livestock. It was something you might have apologised for profusely while still serving it over in Blighty. It was only around the turn of the twentieth century that it rocketed to icon status. Why? The old refrigeration revolution, of course! They didn't teach it at school. It was niche, sure, and not quite as sexy as those other revolutions: industrial, Cuban or agricultural. But that ice changed everything. Once you could slow decay, that rich, oily flesh stopped being a liability and became an asset. And by the mid-twentieth century, sashimi exploded globally – a much needed, glorious bite of golden otoro compared with the colossal bowl of fermented pig shite of events that had been Japan's start to the century thus far.

This was also the rebirth of the fishmonger. Not the ancient coastal trader shouting at dawn, but the modern ones – refrigerated vans, inland cities, fish sold days-old instead of hours from death. Seafood was no longer an emergency, or a coastal rarity. Fatty species once doomed to spoilage – salmon, mackerel, tuna – were stars instead of suspects. And tuna specifically, the big daddy of the ocean, one whose gills profoundly needed movement for life and suffocated from staying stagnant, would become the most consumed fish in history.

Fast-forward seventy years and I was locked in a silent standoff with my fishmonger, who had just handed me three kilos of grey cartilage and called it blue-fin. You probably know the basics when fishing in mongers: clear eyes, bright gills, be suspicious of anything already beheaded. What you might not know is this: like every market stall on earth, they bore a few prize catches on the ice to reel you in, but often the worst stuff sat front and centre, hoping confidence would beat knowledge. And if you hesitated too long, it was already in the bag.

The stare-off continued. As I began to add a little shake to my head movement, I looked around and in burst Tami, like a prophet in a laminated apron. He was my guy, the only monger I'd ever met with a grinning face.

'Hello brother,' he bellowed, flashing a mouthful of nicotine-stained ruin, his thick Middle Eastern accent slicing the pungently irritated queue in half.

He snatched the tuna from the wide-eyed apprentice and slapped it back onto the ice.

'Ah-ta-ta-ta, no. He's chef,' he muttered, like he'd just saved a child from a traffic collision.

Chef or not, I pushed for the good stuff at the monger's

because they had it. They were an odd breed of people. They didn't have a passion for gutting sea beasts and they didn't give a fuck about what you were planning to cook, like a butcher might. Nor did they chat about footy scores like a classic cockney veg-market grocer would. They were clinical hustlers, enigmas of the industry and profoundly uninvested in how your day was going.

'Here boss, as you like it – sashimi-grade,' Tami said as he returned from the back fridge, handing me a bright-red slab like contraband of tuna Akami, middle cut. Blue-fin sushi-grade. It was more a marketing phrase than a legal term but, mostly here, just an understanding not to rob me blind.

Tuna cuts got fetishistically complicated, but you really only needed two ideas tattooed on your brain:

Akami – the top side of tuna and the most common for sushi cuts: lean, clean. The gateway cut.

Toro – the bottom half: the belly, fattier and, on the whole, more desirable.

Within Toro there was *Chutoro* (more of a delicacy and medium-fat, with a literal translation of 'to melt') and *Otoro* (very fatty, marbled and buttery). Otoro was luxurious and where tuna got oceanically expensive. You were unlikely to find it at a walk-in, even in the VIP fridges. Auctions existed for its prize cuts.

To make it simple, I aimed for the middle cut, closer to the head. The tail was cartilage and pushed on home cooks wanting to make poke – exactly what Day-One-Balls over there was trying to flog me.

I grabbed the cut and legged it back to Pauly's kitchen. Time was ticking.

Pauly was an old friend, a childhood friend, a kitchen brother. We'd shared stations, pay packets, blackouts and probably blood types at this point. He was a serious chef, star-trained, but now semi-escaped into private work. I was happy to be his sous or whatever was needed for his events, while taking in all the ropes of private cheffing.

All it took was one solid repeat gig to get solvent. Pauly had struck gold: a weekly Wednesday lunch for a stockbrokers' office, a single service that paid more than a seventy-hour week in a restaurant.

It was 10 a.m. Tuna was sorted, seared, resting. Everything was ready. Nearly. The vibe was off. It was one of those days where the universe had already decided you were about to be humbled. It was palpable.

Neither of us had slept in more than forty hours.

We were waiting on one thing: the dealer. We'd misplaced about three grams of ketamine and it was playing on my mind. I knew that sounded a tad dramatic or even insane, but the idea of cutting off supply now felt even more unhinged.

'I don't care any more,' Pauly declared as the clock hit eleven. 'Let's go.'

It was infuriating, but a hard one to argue. Sometimes in kitchens, there were just days where nothing aligned, and then there were days that were actively trying to break you. One was to follow.

As we loaded everything outside, Pauly came out with several large platters to serve, hand-painted beauties. In the light of day, I saw Pauly's face obscenely cross-eyed. As if written for a joke, he came out declaring 'It's gonna be fine' before dropping the entirety of the crockery down his front stairs. It made a colossal sound, this wave of china breaking and dribbling onto the concrete.

There was a silence, followed by a heavy sigh from the cab driver watching on.

'Fine, it's fine.' Pauly began his self-gaslighting before scrambling for new platters – and two sets of large sunglasses.

We climbed into the cab – neither of us having a driving licence – and whizzed through Green Park. Sitting still for the first time all day, the truth landed.

We'd overcooked it.

Day three of chemical living didn't get you high any more; it just left you in a vacant lobotomised drift. We stepped out of the cab in aprons and suspicious sunglasses, blinking into daylight like astronauts abandoning Apollo 12.

'Fine, fine, it's all fine,' Pauly ticked as we entered reception, crates in hand.

That's when it happened.

As he bent to lift his box, an almighty RIP echoed through the marble lobby.

Pauly froze. His face drained.

'No, no, no, no,' he whispered, not to me, but as if bargaining with a higher power.

'What? What happened? Can you see anything?'

I stepped behind him.

The damage was biblical. His chinos now had a tear from knee to upper crack – which, for Pauly, was a full third of his anatomy – exposing his arse through stretched, exhausted briefs that had long since given up on hope.

Stacey, the smiley receptionist, was seconds away.

'Just . . . don't turn around,' I murmured.

Pauly gulped.

'Fine, fine. It's fine, so fine,' he squealed, as we stepped forward into a glass-walled arena of financial predators.

A man with no sleep, no drugs, and half his arse out, ready to feed the market.

Food was important to these kinds of guys – investors, venture capitalists, PR moguls . . . Eating well wasn't nourishment, it was posture. Blagging taste in food stemmed far deeper than just the plate. It was a showcase, proving that you had taste in everything else: fashion, watches, wives, brandy, cars, affairs and interiors.

We went up to the kitchen of this modern-build office, past abstract art along the corridors that I'd no idea about, only being confident that one was worth more than I'd ever see in a lifetime. Pauly crab-walked with his arse to the wall, nervously over-talking to Stacey to distract from his bum-less chinos.

In the dining room of the office we began laying, with Pauly gluing his back to the wall, desperate not to expose his chef's special, as sweet Stacey returned the small talk.

'I can't wait to get out of here,' she offloaded while setting up the plates. 'I'm drowning in testosterone, guys.'

She wasn't wrong. She was, factually, the only woman in the office.

'I didn't think it would quite be . . . this much of a cliché. One big boys' club.'

Pauly tried to unbox as swiftly as possible while only being seen head-on. I sharpened my carving knife to begin slicing the tuna as quick as I could. The two things you needed to know with fish – sharp and dry, the knife and the surface. The slice was everything, bar searing. The seared crust flaking away from a blunt or wet cut had to be avoided here – some culinary training attempting to shine in a drifting and tranquilised conscience. And if you were on the end of a bender while slicing . . . well, I recommend closing one eye; it helped vision tremendously with the panoramic setting.

The faster we set up, the sooner we could leave – hopefully without any suited frat boys pouring in right now as we felt impostuous, like a couple of fuckheads who dressed up as chefs for a laugh but were in too deep.

In walked Ricky. 'Yes, chefs! What have we got to feed these guys' hangover today?'

Balls. Ricky. He was the first to catch us every week. You could tell the kind of guy he was by the way Stacey's expression dropped anytime he entered.

'Craving seafood, boys. Tell me there's lobby?' He continued to tell us the pricey seafood spots he'd visited in Positano on the Amalfi Coast and how the quality compared to those in Inverness.

Ricky was the prime example. They collected restaurants like shags with Victoria's Secret models. Food was a boast; it was 'I know things and have been places' and a status to afford to care. Your menu wasn't feeding them; it was flattering them, a quiet way of saying their cock was not only girthy, but impeccably seasoned, well-travelled, well-reviewed and confidently swung across the world's finest tables.

'Great menu, today. No lobster, I'm afraid. Tuna and prawns.' Pauly placed his platters on the table as if he was in downtown Kabul defusing a car bomb. I paused, silently praying to anything listening that he didn't trip, fall, combust or experience gravity in any way. We couldn't take that right now.

'All right, then,' Ricky smirked, leaning back. 'Talk me through it, pal.'

Another suit slid in late, arm draped round Ricky's shoulder like an Armani man-purse.

'I'm ready,' he grinned. 'Give me the à la carte, boys. Beluga? – it's been a killer week.'

He winked, then they laughed together, that wet, predatory chuckle some blokes did when pleading for social support with bad jokes.

Pauly placed the platters down perfectly – clean and

controlled. A small exhale passed between us. Even Stacey let out a quiet *phew*.

'Carpaccio with rocket,' Pauly said, lifting the lid of the first tray.

'Vitello tonnato. Prawn and chorizo. Poussin with romesco.'

I could see it then, the effort and strain in Pauly's face, like he was trying not to sneeze, scream or shit himself. At this point, just one would undoubtedly set off the other two, bypassing the chinos with the gaping holes and repainting the antique marbled floor in a diarrheal fresco.

'Not bad,' Ricky muttered, approvingly. 'Not bad at all.'

Pauly reached the final platter.

'And to finish . . .'

He lifted the penultimate tray and stopped.

Nothing came out. No words. No movement. Just silence.

I ceased slicing and leaned in.

There it was: a stunning hand-painted oval platter. Blue fish curling around the rim, Mediterranean moonlight dreams, prancing up into the snowy sky. Wait, not snowy. Three grams of shardy ketamine with baggies were dusted across the artwork.

Time stalled and, for a second, nobody reacted – that rare, holy silence where a room collectively buffered, like the Wi-Fi has dropped and they couldn't load a human emotion quickly enough.

Ricky stared at the platter. Then at Pauly. Then back at the platter again. His face performed several micro-expressions in half a second: confusion, disgust, awe, calculation. A flash of 'is this some chef thing?' entitlement loomed, like someone's just served him a cappuccino in a Sports Direct mug – even though we all knew he slurped from worse.

I had to bite the inside of my cheek so hard I tasted blood. I was so focused on Pauly's full arse not being on display that

I was last to clock. I could feel hysteria bubbling up in my throat – the kind of laughter you get at funerals, when the grief is too big to hold and your brain reconfigures to slapstick.

Pauly looked down at it, nodded once and deadpanned:

'Ketty tuna.'

Once trash fish. Then emperors. Then Michelin. Then whatever regression the fuck this was. We were quietly 'paused' from the lunches: no explanation, no post-mortem – just the corporate equivalent of a ghosting. It didn't last. They loved the food and the replacement chefs bored them. It was a remarkable end message, if not a wrong road to get there. Money forgot fast when it was well-fed.

We were back within months, slicing clean, rehabilitated tuna like nothing had ever happened. We had slightly less toxicity levels but sturdier pants. I supposed history had its way of circling back. Life wasn't all Otoro and truffle. Sometimes it was ketty tuna.

10

Pork belly with miso maple reduction and celeriac remoulade

Serves/8-10 Time/6-9 hours - mostly hands off

Pork Belly, Miso Maple Reduction Celeriac Remoulade

Braising

2-3kg pork belly, bone in + scored
3tbsp red miso paste - mix into 1ltre warm water
250ml White wine
250ml Chicken stock

Heat & submerge el porko

Reduction

2 Shallots, chopped
300ml pork miso broth
200ml Red wine
1tsp chardonnay vinegar
Small bunch of thyme
2 tbsp Dijon
1-2 tbsp Maple Syrup

Syrupy

Remoulade

1 celeriac - mando, then fine julliene
1 Yolk
1tsp whole
1 garlic clove
100ml olive oil
200ml neutral
Juice + Zest ½ lemon
Chives
Apple - fine julliene

Make ahead to sit in flavour

* Braise 5 hours at 120°C

- Trick to Best Crackling
  - once braised, remove skin
  dry out in oven at 90°C for 4 hours.
  - deep fry at 180°C

Dukduk dukdukduk.

A new order on the printer came through. It shot a chef to attention faster than a seagull to a dropped chip.

'Check on, two ceviche and a small tartare. Hold mains,' Karl shouted from the pass.

Dukduk dukdukduk.

'Check on, half a dozen oysters, Bloody Mary vinaigrette, two mac 'n' cheese.'

Huh? Someone on a date pretending to be human up there? What a car crash of a starter; that was one way to ruin a date. Jeffrey Dahmer wouldn't have got laid with that.

There was a brief moment between tickets, I thought, as the clock crept to first bookings. That was what you were subconsciously hoping for: a pause after the printer, just a second – didn't even matter how long, because it represented live time. If there was no pause, it meant orders were stacking and coming through at a faster rate than the printer.

Dukduk dukdukduk dukduk.

'Mains away, on 14, scratch the mac 'n' cheese, two truffle chips.'

That was better – shag's back on the cards for Dahmer – but definitely no pause. This was the turning point of pondering whether to put away *mise en place* and fully commit to service.

Action stations. It was when you felt it, an indescribable rush of energy. Adrenaline started to trickle, releasing a primal focus homed into chest and bollocks like 90 per cent of all things exciting. The orders were going off on one and, as I plated on my section, I sang along to the beat of the printer in my head.

'*Dukduk dukdukduk.*'

On it went. No pause.

'*Dukduk fuckfuckfuck!*'

'Check on! Two Milanaise, three tempura, endive, broccolini, dairy allergen. Let's go!' Karl said, with a raised sense of tone.

'Yes, Chef,' was the synchronised reply.

This was a service at the Plum Gate, back where we started, the pace turned up. But something else was happening to me as the orders gathered speed. I was feeling slow, physically stunted, wheezing and sweating profusely. The printer – it was not stopping but slowing.

Duk duk dukkkkkk daaaaawkkkk.

The kitchen was running circles around me today. We had just had a staff meeting and at around point number three on the agenda, the night manager – in front of the entire front and back of house staff – sternly stated: 'And Ali, will you not do any ketamine tonight? Thanks.' It was as if he was announcing a new cocktail on the menu. It had been reported I was close to unresponsive in the manager's office holding half a bag of shardy powder in one hand and the other submerged in a plate of meatballs.

The request itself was pretty fair, albeit already too late. I felt irked by it. The waitresses turned and smirked at me in pity; the Spanish busboy, who couldn't speak a word, suddenly chose to understand English and gasped. I was back at school, on show and coldly exposed. I wouldn't have normally cared, but he wasn't joking and my mind felt tweaked. Something was off.

I was on thin ice with the manager. There had been a recent incident where I sat in for the doorman along with the bouncer, Liam, a soft, loveable, middle-aged family man and south London geezer. It didn't matter if you were also a Catholic drug enforcement officer – if you were a bouncer, you had the best coke links in town. Period. By 10 p.m., I'd got through so many canned gin and tonics that I looked like the drunk customer perched on a high stool waiting for someone to nanny me home, rather than the person who decided who got entry.

I had egged on Liam the bouncer to sort his coke guy and he caved; the night got out of hand. I remembered brief shots of people coming in and not believing I worked there as I perched on a high chair at the entrance deciding who got to come in. The owners tuned in to the CCTV that night to see Liam dancing on the table in a fur coat to 'Believe' by Cher and me conked out among the jackets in the cloakroom. Liam got fired and I scuttled back to the kitchen behind Karl, with my tail between my cheeks and a guilty conscience.

Dukduk daaaaaaaaaak.

'Check on, mains away on 8. Special request for no ketamine tonight, mate.'

The kitchen cackled as Karl read it out.

'What's next, a double inverted backflip with a side of world peace too?' Mark chimed in. 'La di da!'

Service time was gaining momentum, but it was uphill. I really felt it. The kitchen's banter was hard to engage with right now. I fake-laughed in response, but badly, as I prepped two cuts of bavette steak. I so desperately wanted to seem like I was fine; I always did and I was good at it, I thought. The only thing worse than physical and emotional anguish was everyone knowing. I grabbed my silver cup and glugged. I'd been too anxious to snag a drink from the bar after last night, and so I downed my more recent regular drink of cooking wine mixed with whisky from the nook.

The bitter vinegar of the cocktail went down like nectar at first, but then I retched, dryly but profusely, which was new. I dropped my knife down on my board as I felt tightness in my abdomen, beads of sweat pacing down my face, streamlines rolling through the broken, flaky skin around my nostrils and eyebrows until they were lost into my feral, unintentional beard. I was short of breath and Karl saw it.

'Mark, take over,' he shouted, while he ushered me to the nook.

I entered the cool, silent sanctuary, trudging through the clutter before collapsing on the little red nursery chair and unbuttoning my chef jacket like a wheezing stripper who'd settle for loose change.

'What's wrong?' Karl asked, intensely.

'It's . . . hot,' I croaked out, slowly catching my breath. 'I'm fine.'

'Okay, take your time. We're fine. Coke up top if you need,' he said, pointing to the shelf before leaving to get back to the pass.

I didn't need it. I felt sick. Vomit sick. But I took it, of course I did. I wanted to feel different in any form. Ketamine was the only thing that would stop my recent waves of nausea. I reached into the side of my knife bag in the corner to grab a large, foggy baggie, the last of my ketamine along with a burnt spoon and a pair of fish tweezers; I could smell both on the bag. It was a Q yesterday – the baggie, a quarter litre, around seven grams – and had at best two left in it.

My clammy thumb and index finger slid open the sealed lip and I grabbed my filleting knife with my other. It was a razor-thin knife, but long. I dug it into the large clouded bag as my fingers found focus for a moment, as if my anatomy was aware we had to pull it together. I sliced a yield of around the best part of a gram on the blade and swiped it through my left nostril, vitally keeping the blade side away – an awful mistake to get wrong, trust me. I fed the same to the right nostril. It was instant; the relief was palpable, like swimming too far down and only just coming up for air in time.

I grabbed the coke and crumbled the biggest rock between my fingers, inhaling vigorously while doing so, like chunks of chalk up a Dyson. It was so wasteful. But feeling better trumped any care for Karl's supply. I gulped the nook whisky and it slid down smoothly – or, at least, the sickening feeling was less palpable. I repeated the entire process. Again. And again. And . . . Blackout.

I woke on a floor, with a crooked back and a couple of nostrils more clogged than a Delhi sewer pipe during Diwali – not off-script from most mornings – but there was an escalation that was notable: a depth of physical sickness and an eerie shade of pitch blackness to my memory. I gained consciousness thanks to a high-pitched ring that slowly morphed into focus as I tried to assess where I was. The wooden floor plastered to my face was black, cold and sticky, and it reeked of gin and piss – which could only mean one thing. It was my floor.

As I rose with great difficulty, I saw on the bed next to me my girlfriend, Tracy, sitting comfortably. She darted her attention to me.

'You're up!' she greeted me with force. 'Glad someone slept well!'

I continued to get up, straining to do so. When did I get so chunky? My gut was getting harder and harder to lift off the floor and I was starting to look like Jamie Oliver if he lost the fight to turkey twizzlers. The sugar. The cider. The wine too, I supposed. I forgot if I'd eaten. Those fentanyl Xanax. They were killers for memory. Weeks were passing that I couldn't recall.

'Oi!' she broke, frustrated to not have my attention. 'Are you going to tell me who the fuck is Viv?'

I couldn't imagine what it was like going out with me. I was unreliable, predictable in all the wrong places and often unattainable, but Tracy's biggest demon was unhinged, baseless jealousy. I was far from being the wet dream of any girl with a brain. It was insane jealousy that completely consumed her, whereas I felt sorry for both of us being with each other. I was once phoneless, passed out on my floor from opioids and white spirits. It was bad, even by my standards; I was lying in booze and sick, jittering in and out of consciousness. When she finally got into my house after not being able to reach me and found me in this state of paraplegia, she opened with, 'Where the fuck is she?' As though I'd squirrelled away women under the floorboards, eager for a go on a semi-twitching bloke marinading in the same underwear for a week.

'Well, who's fucking Viv?' Tracy raised the tempo as a familiar interrogation brewed.

'She's my KP,' I moaned.

I could see her paranoid mind putting its own dots together on KP as 'kitchen prossie, kinky pussy'. She was raging, her personality leaving the life in her eyes altogether as the bitter poison took over.

'Uh, the kitchen porter,' I clarified, as I went to the corner of my room in search of a bottle of anything.

'You're full of shit. She texted you for ketamine. Sounds more than a kitchen whore to me.'

Perhaps this was one of those warning lights, a red-flag thing to the rock bottom I'd been naive to. I was now being accused of shagging Viv, the five-foot, mono-toothed Italian gremlin who looked like she hunted Smurfs for a living. This was insane, I thought, as I blindly drank from a stray bottle of wine containing hints of my stale piss.

Waking up had become an endeavour. Continuing whatever this trial of life had become, I was haunted by shame in the first minutes of waking; it was probably the most in touch with reality I'd be for the day in those gruelling moments, as dry, wakening cognitive abilities unwelcomingly attempted to protrude. What happened last night? How did I get here? Sweet, soft Tracy filled me in.

'Fuck head,' she consoled, soothingly. 'You were found passed out with a baggy and a knife again! You promised. Useless drug addict.'

A familiar line, well-versed. It was her end-all statement.

'You're a drug addict.'

It didn't matter what faults Tracy had. Nothing returned an ace shot of an argument better than being told that. Checkmate, Rummy, Jenga, Yahtzee, Junkie.

Shit. I passed out on service, knife in hand. It was slightly better than meatballs, I considered. I drank as the more terrifying thought of the unknown surfaced. I had no idea. Who did I call first? The kitchen was probably raging. Did they carry me out through the customers? Did the manager see? What the fuck was wrong with me?

Tracy was right: I did promise, time and time again – with conviction and sometimes with belief. It was shattering to think she had to live being second to drugs and booze. It was hard to deny, but easy to not confront. She actually was okay with other drugs, but adamantly loathed ketamine – for the same reason I couldn't get enough. I was most removed out of my conscious self with it. It sent me furthest away from the skin I was in, to becoming an unresponsive vegetable.

'I spoke to Karl,' she said sternly.

God, what? He must have been livid. Surely he wanted me gone for ever. Hopeless. It was not fair. Why do bad things happen to useless twats?

'He said, "Don't stress, take some time off." He's worried about you.' Tracy's tone had changed. That was a relief. Although, he was worried about me? That was worse. I was fine, the same as ever. It was easy to deal with disappointment. I'd been a master in the art of letting people down since the first day of school when the teacher asked me to spell out my name. It was harder to be someone who was worried about – especially now, from Tracy. She was a saint for putting up with me.

'Also, give me your Insta login. There are some sluts you're unfollowing right now.'

Ah, that was more my girl.

I didn't go back to the Plum. I didn't have the plums for it. My mind and body were proving overwhelmingly empty and out of steam. People were beginning to look at me with more caution. I could tell my family just didn't know what they were dealing with when they caught a glimpse of me.

My mum was grappling with a harrowing job in the heart of politics by herself and was too honest a person for it. She offered to send me to culinary school in Ireland. It would be 'a ticket out of London for a few months,' she suggested. I needed out – out in any way, shape or form. Out of London, out of this room, out from lovely, terrifying Tracy.

I was suffocating – metaphorically and, after last night, literally it seemed.

I took it. Get me out of here.

Before I left, I sat in Tracy's apartment one morning and I drank on the sofa as she slept, flicking a full deck of cards one by one – a small distraction from feeling particularly sorry to be in my flaky skin. I was banished from the bed, potentially due to her having a dream that a busty blonde sent me a Facebook friend request. I would sit watching my stagnant rolly smoke slowly shift through the living room as the morning light beamed in, surrounded by a flurry of playing cards, numeric and royal, that failed to flee out the window and were now ruined and crumpled on the cold floor. My phone rang. 'Jayyyyyy' came up on my foggy screen. I hadn't seen him in a year, maybe more.

'Heyyo? Is that Mr Gill? Chef extraordinaire?' he blurted.

I smirked, hearing his scatty, mumbling voice.

He was in a bookstore and had seen my face on a book, or so he thought. 'But as I grabbed it, it was your dad!' It was endearing, even though I didn't know what picture it was. I'd blocked anything Dad-related out of my mind the past year. The only control I didn't have was dreams; I couldn't banish him from there.

I bottled up as I bottled down, still struggling to cry, but I would often wake up in floods of tears, from weeping in my sleep. I'd brush past any comparisons to Dad as quickly as possible. I tried not to think about him and avoided it, along with all the other unwanted trimmings in life.

I cut in quickly to ask where he was. Waterstones.

'Wait, High Kensington?'

'One and only,' he replied.

I jumped up from the sofa with a rare rush of excitement and stepped up on the table perched against the living-room wall. I slid the window open from the second-floor apartment. I looked down, across the street to Waterstones, to see Jay in ripped jeans, leaning against the doorway.

'Oiiiiiii!' I screamed at the top of my lungs through my battered phone and across the busy high street while saluting him in my ripped underpants.

Jay saluted back in hysterics, rocketing his empty tinnie into the air. It was a rare moment of adolescent-like thrill, unwritable nostalgia.

I quickly slid into my jeans and yesterday's T-shirt that was crumpled in the corner. I had been loud and I needed to get out before Tracy woke from her slumber. I darted across the high street in Crocs, clothes back to front, and holding the ends of my K cider – no keys or phone. He smelt musky, felt skinny and looked like a battered rock star. It was still Jay. I embraced my old friend boyishly.

We strolled down High Kensington together, with brief pauses of Jay going into a shop and then sprinting out, holding mostly booze and shouting 'Run!'

We were in our mid-twenties and nothing had really changed in years. No, everything had changed; *we* hadn't. It was both incredibly warm and profoundly sad. We walked past the Misty River Hotel. It was boarded-up and covered in graffiti. We didn't linger for long.

The years hadn't been kind to either of us. People swerved around us as we walked down the street; we didn't look like any kind of societal examples you'd want to interact with. There's a point you reach in addiction – a glaze goes over your eye, a lack of care in your appearance and you start to look like an eeriness. Unpredictability consumes you. You can tell you've reached this point when you bring your own booze to a pub garden and you're not kicked out any more. Most waiters and managers looked at Jay and I, and thought: *It's just not worth the pay for the hassle we'd put up.* And they were right.

We ended up in the park drinking from a corked bottle of red wine and eating some stolen chicken goujons.

'I tried cooking pork belly. It gave me the shits.'

I laughed profusely; he had tried cooking straight from frozen.

We used to cook a lot together; not seriously, just as teenagers high on skunk and acid – 'happy drugs,' we'd call them – wanting flavour overloads. Jay's roots were Canadian and he'd always had the most unbelievable maple syrup while growing up – in silver tins, on tap – and we'd put it on everything.

'Fruit! Fuck, on the peaches when we took the sunshine acid,' I remembered.

'On everything,' he said. 'Soup, meat, straight from the tin.'

We chatted on the cold grass for a couple of hours, reminiscing about being younger. I felt old, like the best was so far behind us. We were doing the same shit, but the fun had left the sesh. It wasn't an adventure any more. Something that once felt liberated was now chains.

'I'm glad we're still the same, that we still have each other,' he said out of nowhere. 'I just mean, it's like we were when we were, like it's always been when I see you.'

It struck me and was awkwardly endearing. I knew exactly what he meant. We were the only connection to each other that felt unsullied, even though we had drifted from the days of spending every waking day together.

'I have to go,' I said.

I didn't.

I wish I hadn't.

The joy had worn off and a cold solitariness nestled back into my being.

'Love you, mate,' I added.

He agreed. 'Always. See you more.'

I walked away, leaving Jay in the space where we had spent years side by side: the high street on which we would run from security, the very park where we shared our first hit of acid, and the dens opposite where old junkies showed us how to light dynamite before ducking for cover.

That understanding of free we got from one another, when it all felt so fruitful to a couple of inseparable lost boys.

In truth, I missed it so dearly.

I looked back to see him stay put, with nowhere else to be or even pretend to. He was just perched against the park bench, bottle in hand, looking up to the branches above.

It was an image etched in my consciousness for ever.

11

Soda bread

Soda Bread

1 Standard loaf tin - 9 inch

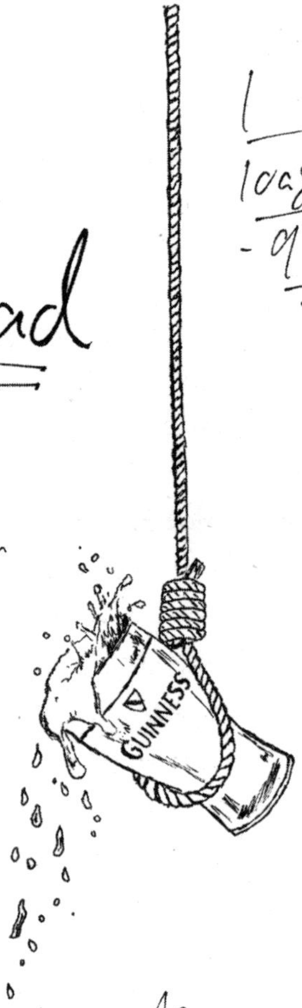

300gr Wholemeal bread flour
200gr Plain flour
1tsp bicarb
Big pinch Sea Salt
2 generous tbsp Black treacle
250mls unsweetened kefir
250mls Guiness

☆ Can sub kefir for buttermilk

☆ Bake 200°C - 10 mins
lower to 180°C - 35 mins

☆ Tap hollow once cooled

☆ standard loaf tin - 23cm x 13cm x 7cm
(9 inches)

Ireland is cold. Not just nippy, but invasively Baltic, the kind that penetrates totally unknown gaps in your clothes, crawls up your sleeves, down your cheeks and squats heavy where few should. I know winter's meant to be cold, but for fuck's sake. I thought there was supposed to be something romantic about Ireland – the poetic masterpieces, the wistful green, the mecca of sonnets and harpsichord dribble. I don't see it. I just see mud and breath. Maybe this is where someone wrote 'In the Bleak Midwinter' and just stopped there, too freezing and depressed to finish. I get Shane MacGowan singing about his town being dirty and old, that checks out. But there's no way Bono wrote 'Beautiful Day' here without heavy pharmaceutical help. Or Ryanair.

I wasn't feeling inspired. Not one bit. I was at a culinary school in southern Ireland, smoking outside the kitchen in one of many vegetable gardens. I was lucky to be here, I suppose. It was a generous and insistent offering from my mother to go do something. Anything. She was lost at seeing me slowly compost in London whenever she caught a glimpse of me. I wasn't averse to hitching a ride somewhere far away, as though switching postcodes could exorcise decades of self-inflicted sabotage. Still, Ireland was somewhere else – and, at this point, 'somewhere else' felt like salvation.

Horseradish swarmed the soil in front of me, its pale roots like a nervous system pulsing through the earth – tangled, anxious, but alive. Plotted around the garden were these large urns, bell-shaped terracotta pots with a single opening at the top. Forced rhubarb.

For those understandably not in the know, forced rhubarb was essentially playing god; it was tricking plants into growing out of season. You stuck the rhubarb under one of those clay bells in total darkness, with just a sliver of light creeping in through the top. It was remarkable, in a bleak *Silence of the Lambs* sort of way. I imagined it's how Buffalo Bill would farm all his veg. The plant reached up desperately for that faint warmth, growing long and pale, tender and confused. It was funny how food mimicked life. Put something in the dark long enough and it'll still grow, weaker maybe, but still reaching.

I took another drag of my cigarette. I smelt a bit like that horseradish.

'Time to lean, time to clean!' a tart Irish tone shouted sternly to me, returning me to the kitchen.

I strolled back into the large, brightly lit space with its clinical yellowish lighting. I was in Kitchen 1 (out of three) with twenty other students. Its uninsulated warehouse room held identical working stations of hobs, ovens and utensils for teams of two, while dotted around in green aprons were the teachers – stern, girthy, no-nonsense Irish ladies. As for the students, they were a flurry of people of all shapes and ages: young posh girls lost after a gap year; older Irish fellas in a tanking business; American spouses sent over here for a break. The one commonality for everyone, though, was some sort of life crisis.

I too slipped into a category here, along with a few other slightly unkempt blokes who had worked as chefs and looked a bit rough around their podgy edges. It was unclear to many why we were here. Or blindingly so.

My partner for the day was Kurt, who fitted into that. He was a chef from Oregon, with hair like Ronnie Wood and good kitchen humour. His mum had just died and what was left was a complicated family; he needed a geographical relocation to break from being a human Pez dispenser for oxycodone. It was good to have him, as at first I felt bitter and demoralised being there. I'm embarrassed to say it – the list of things I should be more ashamed of was endless – but having to endure step-by-step 'recipes' like honey-glazed carrots felt like punishment.

Kurt and I rushed through our list so quickly that it was sport, caring far more for time than substance. It was a pace, a kitchen habit. As everyone put fingers to their printed-out recipe, squinting slowly and reading aloud their steps, we paced as if it were service time, sometimes finishing with an hour to spare, just to make a point.

'Done!' we'd smugly declare, our long list ticked. Mince and cheddar quiche, fishcakes with aioli, chicken liver parfait, marmalade bread and butter pudding. Tick, tick, tick and tick. Fuck me, this was food for grannies, but we smashed the fake hips straight out of it.

'All right there, boys,' said Cheryl, the more brittle-boned teacher. 'Very impressive. Clean down and off you go.'

I carried a bit of culinary entitlement – of course I did. I had as much right to feel smug as a pear-shaped PE teacher beating their primary-school class to the sports-day finish line before gloating how he used to be 'semi pro.' But something new stirred in me. Something almost foreign. It felt . . . good. Fulfilment, maybe? It was oddly satisfying to be top of the class at something, even if that class was mostly made up of beginners who'd never glazed a carrot.

I wandered off, rolling my next fag, when Jan came striding towards my section. Jan was the teacher everyone feared – small, fierce and unmistakable with that bright-red quiff that could be spotted from four stations away. She was the pastry queen of the school.

'Wait there, Mr Gill.'

She began her inspection, her eyes moving from quiche to parfait before locking on the bread, the only thing she ever really cared about. Alongside the ever-changing daily menu, we were required to bake a loaf, a different one each day. Baking wasn't my thing. It felt too obedient. But I had my soda bread nailed – foolproof stuff. Or so I thought.

Jan flipped the loaf over, flat side up, and tapped it twice with her index knuckle. It rang hollow, exactly how it should. But she frowned, suspicious. Grabbing a knife, she sliced it clean down the middle.

'Oh dear, oh dear . . .'

Then, without warning, she turned to the room and bellowed, 'Everyone, stop what you're doing and gather round now!'

The students, young and old, enthusiastically shuffled over; nothing sprites people to attention more than drama unfolding at someone else's expense. My proud peacock plume folded instantly.

'This,' Jan announced, holding up the bread like a crime-scene exhibit, 'is what happens when you overdo the bicarb and don't bother sieving it.'

Okay, now it felt exactly like school – public humiliation, but with aprons.

'There's nothing worse than biting into a clump of bicarb. A beautiful loaf turned to –' she spun back to me, raised the bread to my face and finished with venomous precision, '– inedible.'

Then she dropped my soda bread into the bin.

I scuttled off, pretending I couldn't smell what she meant. But I could. There was a faint chemical sting that tainted the warm sourness inside.

I hated baking. It was chemistry disguised as art. I had five baked goods I could pull off reliably – that was my arsenal, that was enough. Soda bread was one of them. Or had been. Now I wasn't sure if my Wellingtons, brownies or soufflés were even edible any more.

That day, instead of sitting in class for the afternoon demonstrations, I sat in the cottage drinking cheap wine on the sofa, fuming about soda bread and about Jan. Inedible? Really?

I drank until I passed out, snoring on the couch, an Irish version of *Antiques Roadshow* muttering away on the 90s TV perched in the corner. I woke to the familiar tutting of one of my housemates – another bright-eyed student on her dream Irish culinary adventure.

There were six of them in total. Sweet, eager and ambitious, they were the sort who took notes with coloured pens and came armed with more questions than a CIA agent in a post-9/11 interrogation room. And then there was me, the dead fly floating in their cup of herbal tea. Every morning, they'd bounce out the door in their chef whites, bright-eyed and ready for another wholesome day of braising and buttercream, while I was hungover, smoking and trying to remember where I'd left my knives.

I woke up shaking. I was always cursing the cold, pretending that's what it was. But I knew better: this wasn't weather, it was withdrawal. My hands wouldn't stay still. I couldn't get a grip on a pan handle, let alone myself, until I drank. There was no gear here, no London safety net. Just me, a bottle and the shakes.

The worst it got was one morning in class. I'd come in late, dazed from a Xanax hangover, and was trying to peel a celeriac with trembling hands. The root slipped from my grip twice before I managed to slice two clean ribbons across my fingers and palm. Blood welled up instantly, red against the white apron.

Jan was the one who rushed over. She took me aside, calm but sharp, and asked if I was on anything. I denied it; that was technically true, but kind of the problem. She wrapped my hand and told me to go rest. For the first time, I felt like someone had my back.

I grew incredibly fond of Jan after that. People always talk about that one inspirational teacher who believed in them and who, in return, were met with gratitude. I never had that until then. Jan became mine. She was fierce, brilliant and impossible to bullshit, but someone who wasn't trying to catch me out all the time. Most importantly, she was the pastry queen. She taught me how to structure recipes in a way that my dyslexic brain could handle: that pastry mattered more than filling and that baking wasn't chemistry. It was controlled art.

And somewhere in that interlude to my chaos, I fell for baking, obsessively. No one told me how beautiful and meditative it could be: focaccia with olive and sundried fig, white, brown, cinnamon rolls, brioche, soda bread but with kefir and Guinness. We were two total opposites, worlds apart, yet somehow working together. Like me, a Guinness in a cottage full of wet kefir.

After a couple of months, I was steady and better than I'd been in years. I was breathing again. There were even moments of calm, like life had been on pause mid-chaos, and all the weight felt briefly manageable. I think everyone was. We were all in on it – pretending to be functional adults, like toddlers playing 'chefs and restaurants' for a moment. It was structured life and routine. And it was the closest thing I'd had to a real, productive kitchen rhythm in a long time, regardless of it being somewhat artificial. It's funny how quickly the rhythm can vanish. It's held as fragilely as spun sugar and it will collapse with the slightest change in humidity.

There were, of course, still fuck-ups. Naturally, the cracks were still there and the dead space in weekends begged dull after a month. Itching for chaos or some sort of stimulation, Kurt and I sniffed out a coke dealer like two Escobar truffle pigs and charged into Cork one Saturday. We arrived with the other students – bright-eyed, well-intentioned, naive – and almost immediately abandoned them for Ireland's dingiest strip club inhabited by grannies in their thirties, after splitting the cab into town.

'Bro, we should bounce.' Kurt's voice yanked me back to consciousness. I opened my eyes to find myself lying on the sticky carpet of Cork's most aromatic gentlemen's establishment, which boasted both the overwhelming stench of mildew and abandonment issues.

The cab back stank of regret and cut-price Prosecco – the kind they clearly give for free in the private rooms. Kurt was doubled over in hysterics.

'How long were we there?' I croaked.

'Hours, dude,' he snorted in his Oregon twang. 'Hours.'

A sudden spark of sobriety, or panic, shot through me.

'Wait . . . did I . . . with that girl?'

Kurt wiped tears from his cheeks.

'Man, the wall between our rooms was basically made of paper. I heard the whole thing.'

I froze.

'Oh. What did I do?'

He inhaled sharply, then delivered it.

'You spent ten minutes talking soda bread . . . followed by immense snoring. I thought it might even have been her.'

Well, as tragic as that may be, that's not up there with the worst case. Really, the most shocking part? They all agreed it was completely acceptable to let me sleep there like a dying horse.

Bar that, cooking was there again, pulling something out of me to a brighter side. My past culinary knowledge wasn't just spent for Irish strippers. Even students came to me for help. I had purpose. London felt distant and that scared me. Or, rather, the thought of its inevitable return.

Then the end crept closer. Lunchtime gossip started to turn.

'Apparently, it's shut down China,' said Fergie, the queen of rumours. 'The world's next.'

Kurt rolled his eyes. 'Who told you that?'

'My daddy. He works high up in the forces,' she replied, deadly serious.

Christ. There's a sentence that kills conversation. But, it turned out, Daddy from the forces was right. A virus none of us understood was spreading fast, rotting through the world like horseradish through soil.

I was just about to nail my first exam. I could feel it, that sense of – maybe, finally – being one of those students who actually had something to lose, the ones who would go to the library with books instead of the bushes with solvents. But then, of all places, Ireland became the first to shut every school down.

Kurt and I didn't waste time pretending. We found our Cork dealer, bought an eight-ball and two bottles of whiskey, and gave the course a proper send-off. It was unlikely we'd ever cross paths again and we didn't care. The next day, I was on a plane back to London and my dealer was waiting on the doorstep.

Outside, the world closed its shutters. Inside, I did the same. Forced rhubarb without a sliver of light to chase.

Isolation didn't strike me as anything new. I'd been training for lockdown for some time and the rest of the world was only now catching up. For restaurants, it was an extinction event. The industry that had been my lifeblood, my order, my chaos and my clock was suddenly on its knees. Every chef, waiter and supplier was living through the same silent collapse. It was a brutal time for every sector, sure, but few took a hit like hospitality – only the NHS could rival it.

This was the most critical period that our trade had ever encountered. You couldn't plate a meal over Zoom or deliver the warmth of a dining room through the post. While the world migrated online, our craft was rotting without connection: no safety net, no customer service, no understanding of tomorrow. Imagine grafting your whole life to open a restaurant, only for opening night to land in 2020. The government's response was a masterclass in missing the point. They had no grasp of the ripple effect, the abrupt closures, the collapsing supply chains, the tons of wasted food. And those 'helpful' laws? Pointless. The 10 p.m. curfew was a cosmic joke; most restaurants didn't see a penny of profit until past ten.

I'm able to drown any real feeling about leaving Ireland and about finishing the baking sessions I'd come to treasure deeply with Jan – a memorable talent and joyous character who had invested so strongly in me. I possess the most unimpressive flex – a dangerous power and distinguishingly British – to not really dwell on anything, to brush any awkward feeling under the carpet. I didn't let myself feel anything long enough for it to stick. If something threatened to rise sharply to the surface, I was already reaching for whatever blunted it.

Still, perspective had its cruel way of creeping in. People were dying. Others were going mad: shaving their heads, baking banana bread and tattooing themselves for content. Karl, from the Plum Gate, summoned me to the closed kitchen and I started cooking a few meals alongside him for NHS workers. It started as just something to do, some stimulation as we drank, but that quickly revealed something bigger: the real crisis. London's food banks were bone dry. They'd been struggling before Covid and now they were desperate. What began as dropping off a hundred meals by car turned into reopening a shuttered kitchen, producing a thousand meals a day with the Felix Project.

We cooked in vast, monotonous batches: mountains of couscous, pasta, quinoa – shovelling sustenance into foil trays for people we'd never meet. Being a charity gave us a loophole; we could hire, we could move, we could breathe. People were desperate just to be on the rota, a few hours of purpose to break the padded walls of lockdown. It spoke more that most of my friends weren't, however, and were happy with a lockdown – if they even knew it was happening. Jay was the closest and called me every other day saying he was coming to help, but every other day he didn't.

It was a small light in dire times, the rhythm of chopping, stirring, tasting – a heartbeat in a world gone still. It wasn't a cure. It was forced rhubarb; our sanctioned glimmer of light in total blackout.

12

Chicken liver parfait profiteroles with rhubarb chutney and pistachio crumb

Servings / 15-20 pieces

Time / prep-1hr
cook-1hr
chill-2hr

Parfait Profiteroles, Rhubarb Chutney, Pistachio Crumb

Rhubarb chutney

1 large red onion
2 garlic cloves
ginger - thumb sized
1 tsp Mustard seeds
500gr Rhubarb
1 Bramley apple
150gr brown sugar
1/2 tsp cloves, ground
cider vinegar
1 orange - juice + zest

1.

Choux

50g butter
50g Milk
50g Water
Salt
100g flour
2 large eggs

3.

☆ leave in oven for 15 after bake

Parfait filling

1 Shallot
1 clove garlic
1 tsp dried thyme
300 ~~500~~gr Chicken livers
Brandy
300gr Butter

2.

☆ Pass through Chinois

Mise

~~Rhubarb prep~~
(Clean livers) ~~pistachio blitz~~
~~pre prep~~ choux
Apron on
wash

Finish

100gr finely grounded Pistachio

4.

What had been a healthy breather of cooking in Ireland was a blip now gone. It felt like I had stepped off a downward elevator for a couple of months, but the second I returned, I got back on the floor I left and was back on a one-way descent.

Rock bottom is often spoken about like an *event* – a single, catastrophic skid mark across your life that was proof of how far you've fallen, of how morally bankrupt you've become. But, in truth, it's not an event at all. It's a place – a grim little bedsit you can inhabit for quite some time.

I had grown fatter and wheezier, and would sweat in flusters. I felt so weak and tired and was taking more uppers, not just to be able to chop something but to get to my feet in the morning.

I was shaking a lot and waking up – if in my room – represented a painfully sorrowful and long few minutes. Any nightmares my conscience could conjure were dreams of the reality of continuing as I really was. Opposite my bed sat the mantelpiece, a shrine of scattered baggies, burnt foil corners and last night's promises. The first mission every day was the same: an autopilot leap to make it to the mantelpiece before my jittery legs remembered they'd forgotten how to function. Foggy-eyed and barely upright, I'd fish blindly through the debris for whatever pathetic remnants the previous version of me had kindly left for today.

I avoided the mirror. It hung as part of the mantle, waiting, and had become a kind of psychological landmine; a sight too sore when sober, like catching a glimpse of a corpse you recognise. I was struggling to walk now, my motor skills were getting harder to brush under the carpet and putrid acidity sat in my throat like fizzy sour cream left in the summer heat – before I'd even had my first drink.

Why did I feel so sick?

It was hard to really pinpoint. I could hardly remember anything. I shook a lot and I felt like throwing up, which I never do; no matter what I've taken, I'm just one of those dry heavers. This was a new sickness. But because I was feeling like shit 80 per cent of the time, I spent it trying to acquire whatever I could to get back to that 20 per cent.

I had this dealer, Tommy, who ran such a tight operation that one of his drivers could be with you anywhere in London far faster than a Domino's pizza. I would take from him. I'd bullshit as much as I could until bills became so big he'd make me work them off by riding in the car and directing his deals on his phone. I didn't actually mind. It just meant more free produce for me and it was mind-blowing to see that he cleared 10k in a day. (The only shit part was delivering to someone I knew, which always seemed to happen. And there'd be this awkward pause after greeting 'Hey mate, long time. So you stopped cooking then?')

My rock bottom, in a palatable graspable form, was when I became a hindrance to those I thought were far worse than me. Tommy would loathe dealing to me and was trying to push me to seek help. My dealer – who'd done real time in prison, having stabbed his business partner for being late – was now giving me powders in one hand and pleading advice in the other.

I'd become the mad addict to the mad addicts. One night, I

was cooking large rocks of coke with bicarbonate on a spoon, smoking grams alone through a hollowed-out mini bottle of Grand Marnier. That's the way me and Jay were taught to do it as teenagers at the hotel. Crack a hole in the bottom of the bottle and stuff the top with a metal scourer for the rocks; with a low, wide bell-shaped bottom, the mini Grand Marnier bottle specifically had the perfect shape for it.

Whenever I ran out during the night, I followed the sorrowful final puffs by emptying out the charred scour for little lost rocks. By the end of one night in particular, I was pulling apart the same filthy scourer to scrape and stretch for residue over and over and over, cutting my blistered fingers while doing so in jittered desperation. When that ran out, I stumbled to a basement in Notting Hill where a few users I half knew were lighting up.

They weren't happy to see me. They said no. I didn't listen.

I saw a pipe and a blue torch on the mantelpiece, grabbed it, sparked it and inhaled. There was nothing in it; I burnt through the filter, melted the pipe and the room filled with the smell of scorched plastic.

They didn't shout. That was the worst part. They just looked at me, a quiet look of disgust and pity – *You can't scrub with a metal scour.* Then one of them told me, calmly and fairly, to 'get the fuck out'.

I woke up outside my flat on the small concrete landing, half-propped against the wall. I had this *Silence of the Lambs* facemask, the one with the moth on. Well, you wouldn't know – I awoke with it hanging around my neck, caked in an icing of curdled vomit and dried blood.

I couldn't remember how I'd got home – or almost home. But I remembered those looks as the day went by: disgust, pity and that dull realisation that these were the people I'd once looked down on. Worse, I thought I was above them, but if they were at the bottom, where was I really if they were looking down on me?

I started to make pacts with myself, summoning the brawn to face a mirror in anguish.

'No more. One week. Just one week.'

I'd bark it at my reflection, eyes bloodshot, jaw trembling like a faulty motor. And then, blink – time would skip. Forty minutes gone. I'd find myself slumped on the sofa, already half-cut, drugs en route. It was maddening, torturously confusing, like watching someone else pilot my body straight into a wall while I sat duct-taped in the passenger seat.

It dawned on me: what I wanted didn't matter. Wanting was irrelevant. I'd never truly tried to stop anything before, so I'd never understood the depth of the trap I was in. My body was collapsing, crumbling in real time. It would have finished the job too, if my mind hadn't beaten it to the punch and gone completely, gloriously insane first.

I was at the end of my tether, in the space where I no longer wanted to live. And I was too cowardly to end it. It's a space that's hard to dissect. I was too scared to actually do the heavy lifting, to do something about it. I was hoping desperately for something to end it all by itself, for the ground to swallow me whole or an inevitable desire to just take me out, to put it simply. There were occasions when, if the clouds had opened up by their own fanatical chance and excreted a loaded gun onto my lap, it would have been used.

I'd managed, once again, to drag the full beam of familial concern directly onto myself. Turning up at an empty family house at six in the morning with no keys and no dignity, I took the direct route in, smashing the first-floor window like a budget burglar that had yet to achieve enough success to own clothes that weren't stained with cider and smelt of stale chemicals. After realising the smashed window was actually too small, I proceeded to smash the larger window next to it, as early dog walkers scurried past. Once in, I went straight on the hunt for wine, whisky, old Campari . . . anything to keep the night alive. I scoured through the cupboards with bloodied knuckles and blinding tunnel vision.

The police arrived before the buzz did. I refused to let them in at first, obviously. Words were exchanged. The volume escalated. A brief, ugly standoff followed, the kind where everyone pretends it's calm while mentally rehearsing how this ends. Eventually, they backed off.

As they left, one of them paused, looked me dead in the eyes and said, 'You've got no idea how close you were to being tasered.'

I had an inkling, officer.

◆ ◆ ◆

And then one mercy.

My mother. Not just any mother – *mine*. She was a woman built from the sort of steel scaffolding they don't make any more, a support I had ignored and fled from.

She leaned in. It took just one question.

'Are you okay?'

And it was like she'd found the pressure valve to a decade I'd kept sealed. The floodgate burst open – all the pain, all the shame, all the hopelessness that had been fermenting inside me like spoiled wine.

I wasn't okay. Far fucking from it. I hadn't been okay for years. I didn't want to be here any more.

I've done some frightening things. I've been around and used with dangerous people in hair-raising places. But nothing was as terrifying as saying those words to my mum. Reaching out felt like stepping into the abyss.

But I reached and she caught me. The genie was out. She got me to a doctor.

The next day, I was sitting across from a doctor in a sterile clinic near Marylebone. She peered at my test results, occasionally glancing up at me slouched in my chair, sunglasses on indoors, wheezing so loud it drowned out the silence.

'Ali,' she asked, 'can I just confirm . . . what substances have you taken in the past twenty-four hours?'

I began listing them, like reading out a tasting menu.

She nodded, taking notes.

'Right, so no alcohol?'

'Well, of course alcohol,' I said.

'When was your first drink today?'

'Around three.'

She frowned. 'And how did you spend your morning?'

'My morning? Ah. I woke up around three.'

The suspicion in her eyes softened. Then she hit me with it.

'Do you really want to be drinking?'

It was such a simple question and I had absolutely no idea how to answer it. I understood the words, but not the meaning.

Did I want to? Of course not. Except, obviously, yes. But also, no.

I just stared. Slack-jawed and speechless.

◆ ◆ ◆

Dr Tickle – an absurd name, given the circumstances – went on to explain that I was an alcoholic and a drug addict. It wasn't shouted by a furious ex or muttered by a mate. It was a diagnosis.

Clinical. Cold. Final.

She talked about genetics, about how having an alcoholic parent meant I'd always had a 50/50 shot, a flip of a coin. Mine had landed bottoms up.

I could feel the sick climbing my throat, that familiar acidic burn of cheap cider and anxiety. Sweat gathered across my scalp, my face going from dry to drenched in seconds. I tried to thank her, as if ending an awkward chat with an over-friendly barista, but she wasn't done.

It turned out my rock bottom had a trap door.

'There's a reason you're feeling this way,' she said. 'These are symptoms.'

Then the real news.

Early stage cirrhosis had turned my liver into parfait. There was scarring on my bladder, heart irregularities, cracked lungs and, oddly tagged on at the end, chronic constipation. My liver was the headliner, though, the star of the show to her closing act.

'You'll be dead by Christmas if you don't seek help immediately.'

This was something new. A fork.

13

Cow-arse pie

Serves / 5-7   Time / 5-6 hrs

Ox Cheek and Marrow Pie, Vin Rouge Jus

A.K.A. COW ARSE PIE

Ingredients

1.5 – 2kg Ox cheek
Flour for dusting
Oil for searing
S+P for seasoning
Dash of Brandy
— Prep, Season, Sear + deglaze

200gr pancetta
3 large shallot
1 carrot
2 cellery ribs
4 garlic clove
1 tblsp tom puree
— Render, Sweat + season

large Bouquet Garni
400ml full bodied Red
600ml veal Stock
1 tin chop toms
2 tbsp. Dijon
2 tsp. Worcester
1 parm rind
50gr Butter
*Gastrique to finish
— Bubble, Simmer, Braise, Reduce 140°c 4 hours Cool

*Gastrique — Caramalise + Reduce to syrup
- 150gr Sugar
- 150gr Red wine Vinegar

Wrong f*#kin cheek you tw@t!

500gr Shortcrust
1 large egg
1 tbsp double cream
1 large Bone Marrow
— Roll, seal, crimp, wash

Bake 180°c 30-45 min

*Buerre Manie to thicken
- 100g butter
- 100g flour

'Fucking lazy work' is the phrase that swarmed my mind as I sat in this clinical school-like diner staring at a pie, accompanied by an unseasoned pile of bluntly chopped, browning iceberg lettuce. It was a level below a reduced packet of Ginsters. I split the crust from the middle, raw dough oozing a steamy brown mess inside. It resembled ripping open a fully loaded adult diaper that's been flung out in the rain.

Across from me sat Angus, a stocky Glaswegian with a tribal tattoo crawling up his face like a commendable commitment to a life of bad decisions. The thing wrapped around his eye in full Mike Tyson tribute, his expression set in a kind of permanent scowl.

'It's nay bad,' he grinned, ribbons of brown sludge dripping from his mouth. 'Nay bad at all!'

I couldn't tell if it was genuinely awful food there or if the Scots just have a different threshold for suffering. Every one of them seemed to eat like it was laced with morphine.

I pushed my plate towards him.

'Cheers, lad! Love a wee cow-arse pie, me. My mum's favourite.' He mopped up the instant granulated remains with a crust of Hovis, before moving on to mine.

Cow-arse pie – it made me smile. He meant ox cheek. I think. Even though he'd got the wrong cheek. He did call the previous week's meal 'arsehole sausages', but turned out he was referring to the staff who served it, not the ingredients, nor, most relieving, what he was planning on doing with them.

'Don't like cow arse, kid?' Angus questioned me.

It was one of my favourites, actually. Ox cheek, I mean. I loved to make pies, particularly ox cheek, but there's no way you could safely tell me what animal, let alone what cut, was in this curdling slop. I told Angus that my personal favourite is making it with veal stock; it was the secret to a schnitzel sauce at a restaurant I used to work in, which made it fatty and gelatinous, thick and rich. I then spent about a minute trying to get his tattooed head around bone marrow.

He let out a wet burp followed by an even wetter sniff. 'Arse is arse, mate. Just eat it.'

Hmmm, maybe he was right. I was hyper-focused on the food. It was really getting to me; I was pointing a lot of anger at it and I'm not sure why. What a line of Angus's to leave on, though.

He pushed his chair out, grabbed his crutches and hobbled off.

Angus had shot so much heroin into his groin that his leg had to get amputated up to his knee. But even that didn't stop him. He carried on shooting into his groin until they cut the whole thing off. And he was still happy to eat back-to-back arse with valour.

This was rehab, somewhere deep in the Scottish Highlands.

I'd just cleared detox and had been sent up to what they call 'the big house'. Detox is the waiting room of purgatory, a week spent making sure you don't croak before you get a shot at salvation. The place looked like a terminal ward, which is accurate, in a sense. There were narrow hospital beds with an emergency cord dangling above each, knotted and re-knotted by the ghosts of junkies past. Nurses burst in every few hours with flashlights to check your vitals, while the moans of cold turkeys echoed down the corridor. You didn't sleep. You just sat in hot showers, shaking in pools of sweat and chain-smoking. Then, one morning, you're declared alive enough to move on.

I'd made two friends in detox: Martin, an out-of-shape Jeff Goldblum-lookalike who looked like he'd been only partially deflated, and Jason, a stick-thin Canadian literature professor who would stutter but was remarkably sharp-witted. I'd guess they were both on the young side of middle age. It's hard to gauge age in rehab; everyone looks somewhere between twenty and sixty, depending on the lighting and their last bowel movement.

They found me slumped outside in the rain on day two – defeated, disoriented and willing to trade the soaked clothes on my back for anything that might make me feel different. They were a warm presence and felt instantly familiar, like the old friends I didn't know I had. We bonded over our mutual misery; they stated that they too would also exchange my damp underwear for them to get even a flicker of relief.

We were all infants again, grown men being nannied, unable to feed, clean or live without supervision. Our one salvation came when Martin unearthed a battered old Frisbee from behind a hedge. In that week, it felt more valuable than gold, drugs or functioning serotonin. Watching that cracked disc arc through the air became our religion – a hypnotic, stupid, beautiful distraction for brief stints of energy. I wouldn't have traded it for the return of my damp clothes.

Then came 'the big house', a strange, hollow victory lap.

Detox gives you purity by default – sobriety through voluntary captivity. It's like coming out of a concussion. The body clears but the mind restocks, and suddenly all the thoughts you've been drowning for years crawl back up like rats on a sinking ship.

How the fuck did I end up here? crawls to the top.

But even with that, I didn't want to leave. I mean, where would I even have gone? There was nothing waiting. No job, no lover, no life that wasn't already ash. Just an endless repetition of existing, but wishing I didn't.

Family and clinical pleas to be here aside, no one had chained me. I suppose that's key to grasp. I chose this, albeit not knowing what the path meant, and was predominately driven by an apathetic need to continue the charade that I was fine. I just didn't fully compute what that would entail. I felt well versed in profound blues and colossal boredom, but now I was without my chaotic chemical orchestra loudly drowning out the world. Breathing was starting to feel like pernickety admin.

Then, through the fog, as I arrived on the verdant green lawns, came Jason's grin through the old wooden entrance – wide, relieved, alive – a sight of warm comfort during the cold process of being the new inmate.

It's a school reunion special, just for the reprobates, those who've graduated from detox to rehab. A dozen patients of all shapes, sizes and ages sat outside smoking, staring at me awkwardly, assessing the new kid on their playground. It was excruciating and panic attack-inducing, but saved by seeing Jason's smiley face emerge from behind the smoke, marching towards me and embracing me with open arms, swiftly followed by Martin, Frisbee in hand like a knight wielding a sacred relic. They hugged me like a brother returning from war. My chest almost caved in.

'Welcome to the madhouse,' said Jason. 'You've been missed.'

'We've got better,' Martin boasted, holding up the Frisbee. 'You've got some catching up to do, mate!'

'It's not the same with just two,' Jason said, endearingly.

I realised I was trembling, that emotion was trickling back into full colour. It felt new, but the emotion wasn't returning from nowhere. It was that I just wasn't drunk.

No time was wasted. I was straight into a packed schedule, with a fellow patient to show me the ropes. Robbo was a scatty pill-head around my age, which felt a bit like the blind leading the lobotomised. There was a noticeboard with names and classes.

'This is everywhere you need to be,' he declared.

I looked at the dozen pinned-up sheets of papers of diagrams, Excel sheets and the odd inspirational quote you might find in a waiting room at your dentist. It was a blur and hurt my brain to stare at it for too long. It looked like advanced Hungarian physics. I looked to Robbo and, to my relief, I could sense it was the same for him too – and he was already well versed, as well as actually being Hungarian.

'If you hang around the corridor, they tell you which room to go in.'

Robbo was right. I was quickly swept into a meeting by a stocky, baritoned matron. You come to understand that everything must be done together; that the core ingredient to hell is solitary, and so connection is key. But sitting in a circle seemed an endeavour, let alone admitting I was an addict – or, worse, how I was feeling.

During that first group session, something in me wanted to justify why, perhaps, I didn't belong there. A voice was yelling, *Let's get out of here. It's not too late to press the escape button. Just claim I'm in the wrong building . . . Actually, I'm looking for the Highland baking course.*

And then Suzie, a chatty twentysomething from south London with lashes like windscreen wipers, beat me to it.

'I don't belong here,' she declared, chin up. 'And there's times I've had just *one* drink! That's not a problem.'

It was a point. Me too: I could clearly remember a dinner party where I went home after just *two* glasses, and actually slept.

Clive, our counsellor, sober for a decade and always dressed like Gareth Southgate, smiled and stepped forward.

'Aye, is that right? And when was that, Suzie?' His Scottish brogue softened the jab.

Suzie straightened, emboldened by what she assumed was encouragement.

'My son's birthday. I had one glass and called it a night. Even the week before I came here, I stopped after one vodka tonic with my sister.'

Clive nodded solemnly, hands clasped behind his waistcoat.

'Me too, Suzie. September 1983, had one drink, I remember it well. Also, my own wedding day in 2004 – just the one beer, called it a night.'

Suzie blinked, half-nodding, unsure whether she was being validated or roasted.

Clive leaned in, voice dropping like a bag of Maris Pipers. 'Funny thing, though, isn't it? Remembering the one time we didn't drink like lunatics. Nobody remembers having one cup of tea or one slice of toast, yet we remember that one drink. Because for us,' he paused, letting Suzie's grin fade, 'it was the strangest, most unnatural thing we ever managed to do. Memorable, only for an alcoholic.'

It was, by all accounts, an ace return.

I'm not talking myself out of anything here. I caved.

'I'm Ali and . . . I'm an alcoholic and a drug addict.'

It was a start – although, in all honesty, I was clueless as to its actual meaning.

Weeks went by and I grew lost. I felt it more so than others around me, but looking back I'm sure they felt the same, though being able to toss that Frisbee with Jason and Martin was the biggest therapy I could get. It seemed like Jason was trying the most at all of it. He would never miss a meeting and was really attempting the work. But I had reached a point where I'd gone stagnant.

The writing and homework, having to hash out trauma, past relations, having my first drink . . . Fuck that. I don't even remember my first drink. It was in the bushes somewhere when I was twelve, probably like everyone else. But I do remember the feeling of nothing else really mattering.

Group sessions attempted to poke things out, making everything that has been pushed down come to light and seeing how one's life had been moulded through our very addiction. They eased you in by being open with you, explaining that they were the same as you: 'I'm a counsellor here because I can't stop drinking and using drugs,' one stated.

These were odd qualifications, but I guess I'm a chef for similar reasons, Doc. For the first time, I was missing being a chef: the repetition of it; sore soles and feeling so drained that it handicapped decision-making; cooking for fun; the comradery; the worth.

But who was I kidding? It felt so long since I'd experienced fun or worth. It's the same with using – each time a bit of me believed that this time it would be like a first time, when it was all beer, bravado and bullshit instead of benzos, blackouts and bedsits. We weren't allowed phones, music or even books unless approved, so we had to invent our own entertainment. Mine became starvation. Somewhere between the grey mash and overcooked cabbage, I'd developed an eating disorder. So much of my anger towards the place got funnelled into the food, which turned meals into enemy number one. But, more than that, I began to crave the hollow lightness of being empty. It was a dizzy, narcotic buzz that came right before blackout and the closest thing to an opioid I could find inside.

A couple of weeks in, a boy called Teddy arrived. He had piercing blue eyes and a jaw clenched like he was permanently bracing for impact. He was the new entry, but not new to recovery; you could see it in the way he carried himself – half hope and half noose. I was wary at first, but we clicked instantly over bad humour and good music. He had that reserved, almost shy boyishness, which was strange for someone pushing his mid-thirties.

Out in the smoking area, he tried giving me a crash course, the sort of wisdom only addicts pass on, like prisoners etching warnings into cell walls.

'Pink cloud,' he said, exhaling smoke. 'It's like . . . you get a buzz off being sober. But it wears off. Then you use again. Every time.'

It made sense in a horrible way, as if there's a gimmick bonus level at the start of sobriety, a freebie dopamine bundle, before the game really begins. Maybe it *is* like a Michelin star: getting one is relatively easy, but keeping the thing is where lives fall apart.

'Last time I was here,' Teddy went on, 'felt easier 'cos my mate was in too. He could play guitar like nothing you've ever seen. Looked a bit like you, actually. London boy.'

I dragged on my cig, paused, then felt the lightbulb flicker.

No . . . surely not.

'Jay?' I blurted.

'What? You know him?'

I couldn't help grinning like an idiot. What are the odds? Well, probably not astronomical as he's done a few rounds of these places. But still surreal.

'He left early,' Teddy said, shrugging, ''cos he was convinced his girlfriend was shagging someone else at some festival.'

That I remembered exactly. A couple years back, he did storm out of treatment early. And, yes, his girlfriend was absolutely getting railed in a damp tent by some white bloke with dreads who smelt of incense and trench foot.

When I got my phone for the weekly fifteen-minute ration of freedom, I'd already texted him where I was. Almost immediately, it rang. Jay's face grinned back at me.

'You're at ye ol' Scottish rehab?'

I scoffed for a moment, embarrassed and frozen. It was the first time someone outside had asked.

I didn't know how much me being there was a secret; whether anyone knew at all on the outside world. Nor if anyone really cared. But it ran my mind at hyper speed.

'Well, I'm at one, too. Ain't that a shitter?'

We laughed together in relief. Or at least I did. He was more used to treatment, having his family on his case since we were younger.

'I've been to your one years ago. It's a good 'un! I'm proud of you, boyo.'

I felt comforted for the first time while being there, knowing that he was doing it too right now – my oldest pal being on this same shivery, clinical path. And we'd be together back in London. Maybe it would be like old times. Just a tad more stale? Instead of a Scrumpy Jack and a pipe, we'd meet up for a macchiato, I guess.

Whatever, I wasn't alone. The matron came over snapping her fingers for my phone.

'Oh dear, the meter's run out. See you in a couple months.' I finished and turned my phone off.

I dropped fifteen kilos in six weeks. My belt went from the

last notch to the first and still hung loose. I understood then how eating disorders might be the cruellest addiction of all, as you can't quit food. You have to make peace with the thing that's killing you.

There was a girl I befriended in rehab who had been on the edge of dying from bulimia for a decade. She colour-coded her meals: beetroot at breakfast, turmeric at lunch, blueberries for dinner, so she'd know what she'd thrown up by shade. It was efficient, in a tragic kind of way, like colour-coding a filing cabinet of organised pain.

One afternoon, I lay sprawled across the common-room sofa. It was tired-looking, but surprisingly grand considering us, the clientele; it was like the cast of *Trainspotting* had wandered onto the set of *Bridgerton*. Half-delirious, I lay staring at the ceiling. The patterns swirled and looped like ink in water. I zoned out to its hypnotic patterning until – plop – something landed on my lap, jolting me upright as if someone had used a defibrillator.

Martin stood over me, a wide grin plastered across his face.

'Found something for you, mate,' he said, before wandering off.

I looked down. It was a book. My heart stuttered as the title came into focus.

Pour Me: A Life. My dad's memoir.

Fuck. My eyes locked in until they misted as I stared at the cover of my dad smoking a fag.

I hadn't been able to look at a single image of Dad since he died. Not a photo, not even his name in print. I buried him twice – once in the ground and again in my mind – sealing off anything that threatened to make me feel something I couldn't control.

And yet, here he was, staring up at me. It was too late to look away.

I'd never read a word of his writing before. Why would I? He'd always been there – living, talking, filling the room with opinions and wit. When that stopped, I never once turned to his reviews or columns. Truthfully, I'd hardly read anything; dyslexia came bundled with the Gill surname like an unwanted heirloom – and not the only one, as I was to discover.

Now, gripping his book tight enough to bend the spine, a half-empty pack of Camels by my side, I turned to the first page.

I'd always known he was an alcoholic, but not like this. He never seemed broken. How naive I was. He had already walked away from everything I was crawling through: the hallucinations, the shakes, the colossal boredom, the despair that coated every morning, even the same pubs. It was my story, but decades before, by someone I thought I never resembled.

He was gone, but he'd left something behind – a map drawn in his own wreckage, one last bit of guidance. It was proof that survival, somehow, was hereditary too.

I was hooked. I'd never felt anything like it; being drawn to words like these was a totally alien concept. I needed to know everything. I'd sink into the dusty armchair of the library – during breaks, through classes, whenever I could steal any moment – finger to page, tracing each word like braille. His sentences cracked me open – tears blurred the chapters, while I couldn't choke back sudden cackles – all of it hitting with the force of recognition.

It felt like meeting him again. One last interaction had miraculously been stored in a pocket of time in the form of ink and pages for me to discover as I needed it. I suddenly understood the version of him I'd never known.

I needed my dad more than ever. And, in the strangest way, he'd finally shown up.

Very little about my life felt lucky, but that did – and beyond.

The first flicker of spiritual help. I've learnt more than anything to embrace luck as your greatest unbiased ally. Have gratitude, for it's what keeps the luck that falls in your lap.

Each day ended with everyone gathered in the common room, with Tommy – the expressionless, monotoned councillor with the charisma of a parking meter – declaring, 'Can I hear some gratitude?'

Then came the grim little raffle of thankfulness from anyone brave enough to mutter something they're grateful for. It could be anything at all: a roof over your head, ink in your pen, no blood in your stool, a can of Coke – diet, caffeine- and sugar-free Coke that we were enforced to call 'juice' so as to not trigger anyone.

It seems simple, but that early on, you'd have better luck asking Isis who their favourite Spice Girl was. After gratitude time, it was 'birthdays?' – meaning your clean time. Every thirty days is a moment you have to acknowledge. It's a vital recognition.

Silence hit. Then, from the corner:

'Ali . . . Ali.'

It was Teddy, drawling my name like a ghost trying to haunt and taunt. My face flushed bright red, like that of a panicked little schoolboy. He had to be mocking me for something – and, worse, he'd chosen an audience.

'Ali . . . Ali . . . Ali!'

'What?!' I barked while turning to him ready to swing a chair.

'Go get your chip,' he smirked.

My chip? Oh fuck, he was right.

'I'm two months. Sixty days,' I blurted as quick as you might bless someone after sneezing for the second time.

The room took one more beat of silence before it roared with applause. They rushed in, hugged me, ruffled my hair so aggressively that it bordered on assault and embraced me with purpose. It was a moment, a real one. I felt it.

It takes waves to line up for every addict to be given a chance at sobriety. Sometimes it's not even about doing the work or wanting it. My waves aligned in a moment where I became teachable for the first time – and I hold gratitude because, as time goes on, it becomes clearer how precious that is. I'd also have had no shot if it weren't for my closest allies Jason and Martin, and even Teddy. They worked hard and, without debate, stand as good men, deserving of a life at peace from all this bile. Martin relapsed and continued to drink steadily alone. Jason was on a good spell and back teaching briefly, before his final relapse; shortly after that, he died. I know Teddy also slipped and is no longer with us.

It's not a neat ending for people like us. When I found out Jason passed from his nostrils being too burnt out from coke that he had to start injecting it, it made sense to me. I would have done the same. Having to unpack everything in treatment showed how mad we all are. We are those who do not know how to live, burdened with insanity and obsession. Having heard everyone's stories, and telling my own, people like us should be dead or in prison; we're lucky to even get to that point. The odds were always stacked against Jason. Two thirds of addicts relapse within weeks of leaving treatment, but knowing the numbers doesn't soften the blow. It's crushing, trying to make sense of it.

Martin's still going. I hope to see him soon, although that's unlikely as he's on the other side of the world. Sometimes, when we talk on the phone, we daydream about finding a patch of grass somewhere and throwing that battered old Frisbee around like we used to – although Jason was probably right: it won't be the same with two.

I returned to London after a couple of months, but not before having to call family to empty out my room – the cupboards, the boxes, all of it – of baggies secreted in books, bottles tucked behind radiators, and the spoons. The decorative silver set from Mum's collection – the soup spoons, the big Sunday scoopers – were all scorched, blackened and chemically torched to a ruin.

Still, there was a euphoric sense of relief that was undeniable nor fully understandable. A clean slate. A fresh menu. Another shot at life. Maybe it'll be a slice of pie, straight from the cow's arse.

14

Lobster bisque

Lobster Bisque

Serves 6

Time 1.45 hrs

Snag list
- Cayenne
- Fennel
- Bay
- San pelle
- paracetemol
- more maldon

3 Large live lobsters
- Twist off claws + tail after killing
- Steam for 2/3 mins to remove flesh
- Roast + crush shells

3 large Shallots
1/2 Bulb fennel
2 carrots
2 celery rib
3 garlic cloves
1 tbsp tom puree
cayenne pepper

— Sweat down

Stock — 500ml fish, 500ml Chicken

Brandy
White vino

— deglaze — flambe + reduce

Parsley Stalks
thyme
Bay leaf
tarragon?

Finish + thicken

400ml double cream
100gr cold Butter

☆ Blend 2 ladles of soffrito after Straining and return back to bisque

Lobby Soup.. Make it Snappy

Garnish

Brandy Butter/
creme fraish
Tarragon + chives
Sauteed
Lobster meat

London. Six months sober. I was back in my hometown, the place I happily blame as the toxic root to my issues. It was that pink cloud Teddy was chatting about; a feeling of disbelief garnished with the shock of ordering a groundbreaking dish I never thought was on the menu. On paper, I was thriving. But, in truth, I was probably more ill than I'd ever been.

Early recovery is a cold, uncomfortable rebirth, learning to live life as an adult toddler. It's like suddenly the curtain opens to an audience and you're just there holding a trumpet and leading a brass band. *Well, I have no idea what I'm doing here. Am I meant to know? When the fuck did everyone else learn to play?*

An identity crisis was looming over me like a storm with no name. I had an identity as a drunk; it was a shit one, but I kind of knew what I was.

So I went peroxide blonde, wore clothes that didn't feel like mine, exercised obsessively, binged caffeine and sugar, had dating and shagging apps on rotation and tattoos everywhere – anything to drown out who I'd been. Maybe if I didn't look like him or feel like him, I'd drown his thoughts and I wouldn't have his problems. But I still needed a job, some purpose, anything. And I was still a chef. I just needed to push that to the fore again.

Food remained an issue, which is an issue as a chef. It was a bit of control. I had lost my toolkit of substances to numb emotion. If I felt hungry, I didn't have the capacity to feel much else. It got me high, air-headed – I had blinding headrushes if I got up to my feet too quickly.

◆◆◆

Through a recommendation, I landed an interview at Le Brasserie, a relentlessly busy French hotspot in central London. The head chef looked me up and down, like I was a horse he might not bet on.

'I'd love to have you,' he said. 'The grill's full for the month. We'll start you on larder, that okay?'

Bottom of the ladder.

I gritted my teeth and nodded.

In truth, I didn't care. It felt like touching ground after years in orbit. I'd kidded myself before that I was further along the road to 'chef stardom'. Now I was just grateful to be on an actual marked road.

I was nervous to be beginning in the kitchen again; not so much for my cooking ability, but for knowing what to do now that I couldn't join in with all the debauchery, the shithousery, the drinking. What would I say when the head chef asked how many bags of coke I need? I could have just pretended that I'd already picked up, but I hadn't actually seen it since I got out of rehab. I had no idea if I was even strong enough to say no if it was right there, right in front of me.

The larder was quite a large station at Brasserie. There were many cold things to be plated. That's what the larder is predominantly responsible for, while the other stations – like meat or veg by the grills – are self-explanatory, as is the pastry nook in the corner. Larders are mostly for salads, starters and oysters. You'd be right in thinking salads on the whole aren't gripping. But there was one there worth keeping in your back pocket – the endive salad. It was well balanced – bitter endive, sweet candied pecans, sour from the dressing and then a little *woompf*-kick from the blue cheese. And the visuals were everything; it required building like a mini Jenga set.

The cross contamination risk was raised there on larder. In the heat of it, it was a hands-on dish pivoting from oyster, blue cheese and raw egg, and then repeat. Ah, the egg. The breakfast chef left at noon and it was up to larder to take over anything breakfast from then. Some chefs hate it, I didn't mind it. I preferred it to plating salad and buttering escargot. It was by the grills, so more in the action, and eggs were continuously ordered throughout the day, with a large menu offering everything from a simple fromage omelette to an Arnold Bennett with milk-poached haddock. The latter is simple, but you can tell instantly who hasn't made it for a while; there can't be a speck of brown anywhere or the head chef will slide it straight into the bin. And, let me tell you, the shame from a returned dish from a customer is nothing compared to one not even making it past the head chef.

Making omelettes, shucking oysters, deveining prawns, butterflying chicken breasts . . . it all turned anxiety into calm. I was part of a machine again, a trusted cog. The kitchen was clean, tight, efficient – a well-oiled ship of maniacs who'd die for service before missing a ticket. Nobody clock-watched. In fact, they stayed late to prep for the next day. It was devotion to the shift of tomorrow.

The drugs were everywhere in kitchens, that was my experience. I was terrified that accepting the job was accepting a relapse, until I realised they were everywhere because they'd always been in my pocket. I'd sought out altogether more feral kitchens, friends and surroundings before. Atmosphere mirrors its keeper – it rots or recovers with you. A simple formula, once self-pity and indulgence stepped aside. I was even scared of my own bedroom because there were always drugs in there. As if it were a building defect, coke and skag seeping through the cracked ceiling was something to take up with a landlord and not my curation entirely.

It's the little things that become instantly recognisable in a new kitchen atmosphere, the quiet rituals that stitch one service to the next; things like stocktake, a mundane, thankless job that needs doing every evening. It consists of ten minutes spent in the walk-in fridge, scraping off date labels that expired two days ago.

On my first day, the call for who would do stocktake went up and two commis chefs leapt at it with suspicious enthusiasm, a level of eagerness you only ever see when there's a chance to hide from service. The job eventually landed on Lenny, a young commis chef and sweet-enough kid who was reliable yet airy; he was someone who always turned up on time, but without his knives, Crocs and any concept of what actual day it was. He nodded solemnly on being told to take stock, disappeared into the changing room and returned moments later wearing his bright-white puffer jacket, zipped up to the chin and bulging to twice his size, ready for a blizzard. He looked like the Michelin Man auditioning for *The Revenant.*

Without saying a word, Lenny marched straight into the walk-in fridge to take stock.

Now, technically, there's nothing wrong with this. Fridges, by their very nature, are cold; it's practical and sensible. But the way he left the kitchen as a chef and waddled back in as a marshmallow man, with clipboard in hand – it was so surreal, like he was maybe doing a comedy bit. There wasn't a word, a slur or even a raised eyebrow; just the faint squeak of his synthetic jacket rubbing against the door frame.

In any other kitchen I've worked in, that would have earned him a full-scale inquisition – or at least a volley of creative abuse. But here? Nothing. Just quiet acceptance.

It was oddly refreshing, like watching a baby seal wandering through a minefield and somehow making it to the other side.

Kat, the sous chef, ruled the kitchen. A large, stern German woman who never cooked, only commanded, she was like an SS version of Miss Trunchbull from Roald Dahl's *Matilda*, barking through the pass.

'Nein! We'll be here 'til Christmas slicing flanks like that!'

Or, 'Sharpen your knife. It's blunter than your brain!'

After a few weeks, I started a night shift with Rollo and Leo on the grills. They were both Italian: one was all style and tantrum, the other all noise and no rhythm.

Leo was brilliant, but haunted; he had Michelin-starred PTSD, the kind where fear calcifies into rage. Rollo was a loud, charming liability, the kind of chef who could lose a ticket and blame gravity.

And there I was, six months sober, hair like bleach and static, finally feeling steady on the line – somewhere between reborn and combustible.

As I diced shallots for steak tartare, I went into a sort of dazed autopilot for what I felt would be an unstrenuous shift. That was until the German presence creaked down my neck.

'Allo, mein Slim Shady.'

It was brutal but expected, what with me being in a kitchen with peroxide hair – a step up from Machine Gun Kelly.

'You're on grill tonight.'

'Oh yes, Chef. Rollo?' I stuttered for a moment.

'Rollo is gone, useless. Try not to fuck up. You have some tiny shoes to fill. Go debrief with Leo.'

This was also a moment for Lenny, the young commis. He was to lead the larder pass in my stead. I gave him a quick rundown of the station, the *mise* that needed topping, and how to plate the lobster-bisque special, before showing him once more how to quenelle the brandy butter without it looking like toothpaste squeezed by a toddler or as if a seagull had just flown over the plate. I packed my knife bag and slid down the grills.

Bertie was on expeditor, the last line of defence between kitchen and floor. It's a job that predominantly belongs to the head chef, but ours was strictly a daytime sort of general. Bertie, though, was a Slovakian specimen built for the task: unflappable, sharp and uniquely serene amid chaos. Expediting looks simple, until it isn't. When the orders stack and the printer screams, it becomes a mental warzone. Having a good expeditor is the difference between ballet and butchery.

'Good luck, brother. Don't forget to turn the grill on,' he smirked through a goofy grin.

Humour wasn't really his forte.

Service hadn't even started yet, but I could already feel it pulsing through my veins like a first high, only sober.

I walked up to Leo. I'm six-three, but still had to look up at him, all limbs and bones, a scarecrow in chef whites. He was already pissed off. This wasn't what he'd signed up for.

Leo was used to greatness: structure, precision and teams so polished that they could plate rabbit offal twelve different ways without breaking a sweat. He was on the grill, prepping his section and barking instructions without even looking at me.

'All right, Chef. Only twenty steak Dianes and they're pushing the sole upstairs so expect it. You're also on kedgeree and all sides. Stay awake. We've got 180 covers tonight – it's gonna be non-stop.'

'Yes, Chef.'

I'd already forgotten the number of Dianes, but there was nothing else to say. He was a lit fuse and I wasn't about to hand him the match. He was right, though – it *was* non-stop. A record night: more than 250 covers.

The printer didn't pause for a breather all service – and neither did we. There were a good couple of hours where the sliding ticket holders in front of us held half-a-dozen orders and we were competing just to keep the ticket rail at capacity – as one got spiked, a new one came in. Leo moved like a pissed-off ballet dancer – precise, violent, but beautiful in his own way. And I was desperate to keep up.

'Entrecote! Two Holstein schnitzel! Two fries! Mains away on four!'

Each shout was a gunshot perfectly rhythmed and fired with remarkable accuracy to my gut.

A ticket will often come in stating starters and then what the table want for mains, but it will say HOLD. You need to hold on to the tickets until the waiter sends through 'mains away', signalling the table is ready. It's worth noting as it can usually be host to the biggest cock-ups.

Leo shouted the mains away. I looked to the ticket: two portions of spinach from my section: easy. Then, DAIRY ALLERGEN. Also, no stress as there was very little dairy on the sides, while the spinach just required a dip into the bain-marie on my section before plating and sending, which I sent with ease.

The thing about service is that small fuck-ups in the kitchen can become catastrophic in the dining room. Knowing your food – *really* knowing the path that all the ingredients have passed to be plated – can be the difference between a happy customer and a corpse. But spinach? Fine. Right?

That was, until I turned and saw Lenny.

The little baby-faced bastard was rinsing his cream-covered spoon in my bain-marie.

'What are you doing, Chef?' I stuttered, my brain lagging behind my horror.

'Just two more bisques working, Chef,' he said, blissfully unaware he'd just weaponised my section.

'Kedgeree! Wake up!' roared Leo, and I was spiralling.

I plated the kedgeree, balancing two eggs on top while my mind detonated. They'll probably be fine, I thought. Dairy's usually intolerance- or trend-based, right?

No. This had to be fixed.

'Chef! Spinach, table four needs to come back! Allergen issue!' I shouted to Bertie, the expeditor.

'Okay, relax,' he muttered, squinting at tickets.

'Spinach table four,' he read out. 'Allergen crustacean.'

Fuck. Shellfish too. Lenny's spoons were undoubtably marinated in lobster bisque.

'Lenny! How long have you been using my bain-marie?'

'All night,' he said, wide-eyed and smiling like he was showing off his ineptitude.

My heart plummeted.

Someone upstairs was about to die. From spinach. *My spinach.*

'We need to get that back, NOW!' I bellowed, sprinting to the pass. Leo muttered something in Italian that sounded like a prayer or a curse.

'Hello?! The spinach! It's an emergency!' I continued, raising the volume to dire.

Tickets fire-blasted through for the same table.

Spinach table 4 – ALLERGEN PEANUTS
Spinach table 4 – ALLERGEN GLUTEN
Spinach table 4 – ALLERGEN SESAME
Spinach table 4 – ALLERGEN SULPHATES
Spinach table 4 – ALLERGEN CELERY

'What the fuck is this guy, a rice cake?'

Everyone was staring now – the KPs, the grill, even pastry. The kitchen stopped. Then one final ticket printed.

Spinach table 4 – ALLERGEN SPINACH

I blink.

'. . . What?'

At that exact moment, the head waiter, a greasy Parisian apparition, burst through the doors holding a silver side plate.

'Pardon, Chefs! Ignore! All table 4 – allergen test for new junior!'

He slid the plate across the pass with the same blasé detachment you'd expect from a Frenchman dishing out rations in a siege.

Bertie picked up the spinach with tongs, held it to the light and screamed: 'Run for your lives. It's radioactive!'

The kitchen erupted. Laughter rippled from KP to grill to pastry. Even Lenny was cackling, the stupid bastard.

Relief hit like morphine, then a cold shudder of embarrassment quickly brought it down. Seeing that limp spinach dangling from Bertie's tongs, I suddenly felt like the intern who'd called a bomb squad over a lunchbox.

My panic felt so reductive. I was the butt of the kitchen.

The service trickled to a steady halt and last orders finished at 11 p.m. on the nose. I quietly cleaned down my section as the rest of the kitchen conversed loudly. I felt alienated – even more so when the after-shift beers came out. Bertie came round to my side of the pass, where I was scrubbing the inside of my fridge drawer, and handed me a cold bottled beer. It was a bridge, a connection, a way of saying 'it's all good', which I had to deny.

Each instance of saying no to booze was meant to be a huge victory. But it didn't feel good. This looked different. In the way the beads of condensation ran down the brown glass, it looked like godly nectar. And I must have looked like a cunt for saying no. But Bertie just shrugged and continued offering to happier people.

I bet it tasted different.

After I cleaned down, Kat pulled me aside.

'Great job tonight. You made the right call and gained the nickname Spinach Killer. I'll keep you on grills more often.' And she did.

That felt good, like the first time I had really stepped up in years in a kitchen and been recognised. God, it felt good to feel knackered, to have the thoughts drained out of you, and being sore from the soles of my feet right up to where I have to hunch my back to slice on the tables that were meant for chefs four inches shorter.

The chefs went on to the midnight bar to drink. I went home to log into an AA meeting. There felt the difference now between me and the rest of the kitchen.

I imagine that, if I weren't this alcoholic, I'd drink to that every day.

15

Lapin à la moutarde avec escargots (rabbit in mustard with snails)

Time 1hr 45min

Serves 4-6

Lapin a la Moutarde, Escargot

Team Rabbit

1 whole Rabbit - Jointed
100gr Butter
2 large Shallots } Sweat
1 tbsp flour
200ml dry white Vino
150gr Stock, chicken
Thyme Sprigs
Bay leaves
3 tbsp Dijon + 1 for finishing
200gr double Cream
1 tbsp crem fraiche
Microherb & Parsley for finish

Team Snail

1 can cooked Snails - 200gr apox
200gr Butter
50gr parsley, trimmed
3 cloves garlic
1 tsp white wine Vinegar
Heavy pinch Salt
Olive oil to loosen
2 tbsp breadcrumbs
Lemon

Blitz 4 G. Butter

A low on hob for 1 hour

A whisk in Dijon & zest before serving

A Serves well with puree & biter leas
- Punterelle
- Radichio, Endive

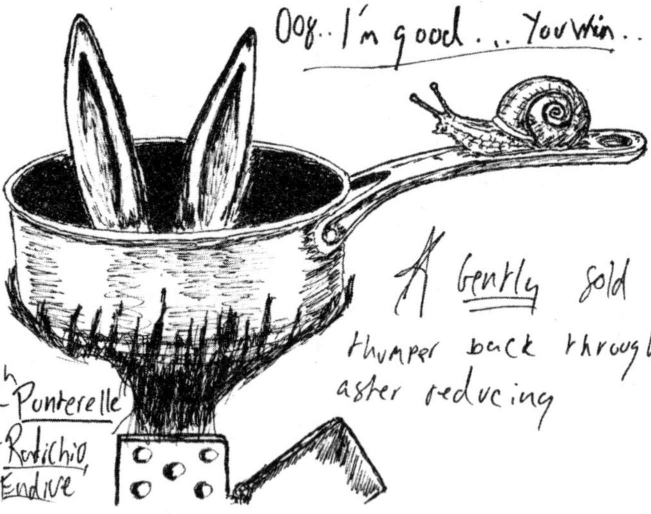

Oof.. I'm good... You win..

A Gently fold thumper back through after reducing

'Milestone slaps' in recovery are moments that happen serendipitously. They're 'higher power moments' – instances that beam the understanding of identity, and gratitude of your waves lining up to something new. They can hit you right across your face, invasively, like someone swinging a fish and slapping you bass to mouth. They can come in ridiculous moments of understanding the insanity and the reality of the tragedy that's unavoidable in addiction. Also, hilarity; moments of being able to laugh with a fellow degenerate about the horror stories, when they don't feel too close to the flame.

One of the first real slaps in early sobriety came when I ran into someone outside a meeting.

Ricky East. Yes, *that* Ricky. Remember him? The crack-addicted, hotel-basement philosopher who taught me why rotten teeth don't bleed and who rolled joints that violated every known health code; the old boozer who showed how to hollow out a mini Grand Marnier bottle for a survival pipe, like a junkie Bear Grylls. I would've bet any amount of money he'd died, been buried and probably resurfaced as compost at an all-girls boarding school.

But there he was: alive, upright, even vaguely pink-skinned. We hugged – properly hugged, the kind of hug that knots your throat in sheer disbelief. Seeing an old using-buddy on this side of the wall felt nothing short of miraculous, like spotting a ghost who decided to come back as a tax-paying citizen.

And, of course, the universe keeps things balanced.

Sobriety also dishes out the other kind of slap.

One day, not long after that meeting – and literally minutes after thinking about a close teenage friend I hadn't seen in years – I spotted this very friend slumped on a pavement, hands cupped for change, almost unrecognisable. Same city, same street, same disease – just a different chapter.

I crouched down, said his name and when he looked up, the years fell away. Poor bastard. The three of us – me, Ricky and this old friend – ended up coagulated in the same meeting soon after. It was a strange trinity: one climbing out, one clinging on, one sinking fast.

Sobriety isn't linear. It's a series of slaps, some that wake you up, some that break you down and some that remind you exactly how thin the glass is between the living and the lost.

◆ ◆ ◆

When I left Scotland, I loathed the thought of feeling like a patient back in London and bringing the *One Flew Over the Cuckoo's Nest* live action I'd been living in Scotland back here. I wanted nothing to do with it, and insisted that I was fine by myself. But, as with most of my predictions, I was wrong – and suffering for it. I was in an obvious crisis, although nothing is an obvious crisis after a life as a drunk. But there was an uneasy, hollow danger, like a cast-iron pan on a hob full blast with nothing on it, just gaining heat and smoke, without sustenance or purpose.

A couple of months passed and I was sitting opposite Dan, my counsellor. He was part of a halfway house, one designed to ease you back into life after treatment. They had tiers: full-time, part-time, day patient, night crawler, day walker . . . you name it. They're flexible for the undead merging back to life.

I agreed to see Dan weekly. He was something of a figure in the world of recovery; everyone seemed to know him, mainly because he was at the mouth of the river when coming through treatment. And so many passed through him. If he shared at a meeting, you remembered it. He didn't feel like a doctor, a therapist or a teacher – just an old cockney West Hammer who enjoyed a crude joke and a partner half his age. That's the difference with shrinks for addicts and ones for your average midlife-crisis Joe. They are mostly addicts themselves, still fighting obsessiveness while getting it right and wrong just as any other drunk.

Dan, for example, had just taken up smoking in his late sixties, past the age that Dad was before cancer took him. When I called him mad, he replied, 'I had to choose between a drink and a roll-up. I chose the roll-up. It was a close call.'

Well, he chose right. But it was harrowing to hear that it never ends, even with decades of clean time. You still bargain with yourself to gain a day of sobriety.

The room we met in looked like a teacher's office in a primary school. There were corkboards plastered with thank-you notes and wobbly drawings that could have been done by children, except they weren't. They were by grown men trying to spell 'treatment' in crayon. Better than me, for that matter.

Dan dropped into his chair opposite me with a sigh and a grin.

'Right then! Let's give this another go, shall we?' I was testing his patience. The week before, he'd ended our session saying it was beginning to feel like 'pulling teeth.' It caught me off guard; I thought we'd been doing all right. We talked. I stared at the clock a bit, but I wasn't completely silent.

'So,' he said, leaning back, 'what's been happening this week then? How's the cheffing?'

I was jittery, on edge and feeling incredibly uncomfortable in my seat that week. I'd bitten off a lot. I was still cooking and thriving, I guess. I was in a relationship – which, according to the rulebook of early recovery, you're definitely not supposed to be. We'd moved in together within two months of meeting, that was probably why. I was spiralling. I was empty and whatever was still under my ribs was rattling loose – and I didn't know how to hold it together.

'It's my fucking car permit,' I blurted out, in a nervous fit.

'Ah, right.' Dan leaned forward, squinting with intrigue like a detective out of his depth.

'I don't know what the fuck to do! How are you meant to do these things? They make it so hard. I'm fucked. Totally fucked!'

My hand that had been casually holding my head like a stress ball started gripping harder, so hard that I nearly pulled out a clump of hair. My eyes watered, not from sadness but from sheer, stupid frustration. I was never good with this kind of thing: forms, numbers, logic. I was running way past capacity.

'Okay, it's all right, Ali,' Dan said softly, trying to soothe the combustion across from him. 'You're doing fine, son. These things can be headaches, but car permits are usually sortable. Where are you living again?'

'It's not, Dan. It's *so hard*.' My face tightened, my voice half-growl, half-plea.

'I'm still in Farringdon, but what if I move back to Hammersmith?'

'Well, then,' he said, 'if you do move back, you get refunded for the year. Then you apply for Hammersmith.'

'Really?' I looked up, a flicker of hope cutting through the static. That didn't sound so bad.

Dan shifted, raising an eyebrow, leaning back slightly.

'Where's your car now?'

'As in . . . right now?'

'Yes. Where's your car right now?'

'Oh, my car.' My trembling steadied for a moment, as I reached into the kicked hornets' nest of my mind for an answer.

'I haven't got a car.'

I'll never forget the way Dan's eyes widened.

What *was* going on? I was completely lost. The confusion hit harder than half-a-dozen grams of horse tranquiliser ever did.

I didn't even have a licence. Hardly started lessons, already hyper-fixating on the future: how I'd flee, where I'd go.

This was one of those milestone slaps. The ones that sting, but wake you up.

I was stunned.

Dan began to snigger and rolled into an all-out laugh, which triggered me into laughing anxiously, like an unhinged madhouse patient with pulled hair that looked like I'd just attempted to debone an electrical socket.

'Okay. How are the meetings going? Your step work?'

I loathed this. It was like being riddled on your homework.

He meant AA and NA meetings; I wasn't doing many. The recommendations were overwhelmingly constant, with meetings and sharing every day at first before regularly doing at least a couple a week from then on. Then the twelve steps. I'd done the first three in rehab:

Accept you are powerless, that your life has become unmanageable. This is the hardest step for any addict in life, but a pretty easy one for any addict at a rehab. It's tricky to fight for your cause of a manageable life when you've ended up in a place that checks your arse crack and piss for gear.

Come to believe that a power greater than ourselves could restore us to sanity.

This was harder to grasp, but the word 'come' was the key part for me, most importantly taking me out of the driving seat. Because, as we know, I can't drive.

Make a decision to turn our will and our lives over to god as we understand him. I was told misinterpreting 'god' is the great stopper of many addicts getting clean. I get it: it's such a blinding word that it blurs out the most vital 'as we understand him' part.

I'd got a sponsor and had done the three again. And then I changed sponsor and was up to Step 3 once more, but stalled again. I was literally doing the three-step waltz – 1-2-3, 1-2-3 – and was stalling at Step 4, the work to do with your sponsor to gain 'spiritual awakening'. It's an off-putting phrase, but is the sought-for key to maintaining everything, to achieving a clean life. And step four is where things get testing.

'You're empty right now,' Dan shared. 'You've got the answer, but no idea about the question or what to do with it.'

I took a deep breath and composed myself.

He was right. I was lost. Scratch that. A mirror had just been lifted to the insanity of my projections.

The problem wasn't substance. The problem was me.

It had always been me – a gaping black hole inside that believed something outside of me could fill it. I'd had a sponsor that I avoided calling at all costs. He was an Old Testament kind of addict, the kind of sponsor who's ideal for the slow ones: fully inked-out, gay, right-wing, American. He had told me the exact same thing Dan was spelling out, only in better words and in his camp East Coast accent: 'You know what you get when you take the rum out the fruitcake, Ali? You know what's left? Still a fucking fruitcake.'

That was a good one. I should call him.

Dan continued, 'You need your Step 4 – *make a searching and fearless moral inventory of ourselves*.' That's the beginning of healing. He went on. 'It's a programme of action and work, only if you work it. I can't tell you why it works, only *how* it works. But work it does.'

A programme of action.

It was a lot. Too much – writing down all the things. All I saw were words and numbers. The discomfort was skin-crawling; what a cruel task to be assigned while sober from the only emotional healers I knew. I couldn't help but think I was forever destined, naturally, to be on my own. Doing this – all this – felt like twisting my arm to the point of snapping into splinters. I didn't know why. It was so uncomfortable to engage and connect, but the hitch was that the wool had been pulled now. The great truth any addict has to comprehend is the understanding that it's against an alcoholic's nature to be sober, that rewriting what was destined doesn't happen for all of us.

Still, though. What happened to one day at a time?

I blurted out what was sitting on my mind now that the car permit had been put to one side.

'How are you smoking?' I asked. 'Does it never end? The discomfort? No peace?'

Dan sniggered. 'Of course I get fucking discomfort. That doesn't collide with the fact that sobriety has given me a life beyond my wildest dreams. I wanted a drink last week and I stayed sober. Isn't that remarkable from where we both used to be?'

It was, when put like that. Another lightbulb-slap moment.

I'd always associated 'hard' with 'not worth it'. But when I thought about it, my life was easy when I was a using addict and I wanted to die. Maybe a hard life of sobriety was the key to the kingdom. I haven't read all of the AA book – only the parts I've been told to – but I remembered one line: 'I traded in an empty bottle and a hangover, in return I got the keys to the kingdom.' Though not in reach, it felt less corny now.

I looked to the clock for the first time in the session. I hadn't glanced at it once and I'm usually fixated on it. The time was up and my shift started in twenty minutes. I grabbed my bag with my knives and got up.

'It's gonna be okay. Thank you, Dan.' I tried to tie things up, my head now somewhere else. But Dan offered his most useful line to me.

'Hold on, hold on. It's not *gonna* be okay. It actually is okay now. What you're feeling is reasonable to what's happening. LIFE ON LIFE'S TERMS!'

It seemed like a nothing sentence, but was at the core of so many inherent problems as both an addict and a Brit. My constant response to the need to survive was to project that it was *going to be* okay and not addressing the current state by sweeping everything under the carpet. Get on with it. Don't make a fuss.

And, in that instance, there was an understanding that not being okay was okay in itself. Fuck me – it wasn't quite like I'd discovered fire, but close . . . the first neanderthal sparking a fatty. It was the acceptance of life on life's terms, the letting go of trying to control everything. That's what the higher-power mumbo-jumbo is at its core. I'm not in charge.

'You're white-knuckling,' Dan concluded. 'It will get painful. We only do this together. See you next week.'

I hugged Dan that evening. It had felt real, a reflection of what I was: still sick and broken. I hadn't kicked anything. White-knuckling is an expression used for being a 'dry drunk', for being sober, but one that was spiritually empty for not being a part of healing or caring to understand why we drank.

I needed to do more.

I ran out, through the deep plume of smoke from the new addicts clouding the exit, and through the bustling underground at rush hour into the restaurant.

In terms of survival, times were feeling tenser at the brasserie.

We had become hugely understaffed, with chefs hard to get hold of post-Brexit and now post-Covid. All the foreign workforces had gone home and there wasn't much reason to return. The English dream of work was becoming a farce and, absolutely most detrimentally, there was a growing atmosphere that this country didn't want them here.

This meant there was also a rise in agency chefs. We had to hire two or three every day to help out on prep, but none of them wanted a permanent job because they were being paid more than the sous chef for the day. It's ultimately unappealing for them, though. We put them on the worst jobs and they were never really part of a kitchen as one.

Upstairs, the front of house was suffering too, especially as someone had to be moved due to John Cleese coming in to dine with a broken leg in a cast, and the waiter just couldn't hold in a Ministry of Funny Walks gag. Respect to him.

I dashed through the weighted rouge drapes at the brasserie's entrance and strode across the sleek, marble checkered floor. I was five minutes late on the kitchen floor, which means thirty minutes late to the kitchen. Early is on time, on time is late, and late is unacceptable. The German was ready to crack her whip.

'Ah, morning, Chef. Wakey wakey. Late from the pub?'

Nope. I was at the halfway rehab on the verge of combusting about a car permit for a car I don't have.

'Yes. Sorry, Chef.'

I'd take being late at the pub; nobody knew why I didn't drink after shifts. Overdoing the pub felt more understandable from a kitchen stance, like the unwritten rule of how smokers get considerably more breaks.

'You're on grills with Leo tonight. But, before that, you can start with putting on the veal stock. Good boy, Chef.'

'Yes, Chef,' I sighed.

Oh good, the veal stock. She'd done it as a dig: gathering half a dozen full calf legs from the fridge and marching them down the kitchen. Their gelatinous rubbery calves bounced and jolted with each paced strut. It wasn't so much the gruesomeness of handling them. It was more about having the extra job, which puts you behind *mise en place* on your section.

No matter how many times you see it, there is something slapstick about the full calf legs bouncing at the knee as they're carried. I gathered all the fatty legs, my chef whites now imprinted from where I'd hugged them. I put them into the eighty-litre boiling pan with vegetable cuts and placed the lid on to slowly cook. It's a remarkable piece of equipment; huge for batch-cooking at a steady rate, mainly for stock and for slow processes, such as onions to make onion soup. It's electronic with an up-and-down button that will tip itself forward to empty if you wish, sort of like a chair in an old people's home that electronically tips out your nan.

I sorted the stock and smirked as I momentarily thought of Angus, the one-legged Glaswegian junkie from rehab – and his cow-arse pie, for which I'd told him to use veal stock. The thought of him walking – or hopping – away from rehab thinking he was gonna do what I'm doing now was a longshot. I hope he's thriving. I doubt it.

Mise en place raced and wrapped, and service slid into that rare, deceitful early cruise.

Lapin à la moutarde was on the special: rabbit in mustard

– a peasant classic dressed up for Chelsea appetites. The escargot butter that we pipe all day – a garlicky, parsley-green sludge capable of resurrecting even the most pensioner-grade baguette – sat calling to me from the corner of my board.

In a kitchen, you're only hunting for quick bites – and mainly forced to, for energy not appetite. I don't think I've sat down for a proper meal on a break in my entire working life. But that day I smeared snail and butter across the rabbit flesh, shoved the whole Frankenstein assembly into a torn hunk of baguette and inhaled it like stolen fuel.

Dad once had a dish named after him for insisting on having escargots piled on top of his entrecôte. So there I was, eating my own version – the fastest and slowest creatures in France, finally united in the same sandwich.

Some kind of poetic symmetry came with this lapin-escargot sarnie: a sprint and a crawl, the slow one cooked fast and the fast one cooked slow – and stuffed into a single mouthful, for my own stamina.

I was somewhat distracted, but also levelled; even Leo wasn't yelling his normal profanities with such aggression. I'd earnt a bit of his respect, which felt good, but I was aware it was totally perishable with just one lost ticket. I locked into service, but I was thinking of Dan. That session felt different, like there had been movement, a Step 4: why was it so fucking hard to do what was good for me? Still, what was that? It was like there was another conscience that always wanted to get me alone, cut off.

Lenny, the commis chef, approached. 'Chef, I'll up the onions, if that's okay? It needs topping up.'

'Go for it,' I replied, blazing while racing through the steaks on the grill.

I don't know why I'd fought to be by myself for so long. I'd cut off so many who were close to me, perhaps for reasons of trust or lack thereof. And the lying. It was exhausting. I hadn't had such close, honest comradery or support before. Other than Jay, maybe.

Fuck, Jay. How had we not seen each other since our treatment? I know he'd stayed in the countryside and was now under a counselling eye. I guess it was a bit like the halfway house. But he should be back in a couple of weeks. It was a bizarre thought, being on this side of the wall: whether it would be good or bad; whether we'd bring each other down or have each other's back. I guessed it couldn't be worse than the state we were in. Last time we met, we were wheezy and sweating like onions, like some awful band reunion with the stars looking used and diabetic.

Onion? Is that what Lenny just said to me? What onion?

I paused for a moment after taking two bavettes to rest. I heard the low binary hum of the boiling pan being tipped. That wasn't good. I looked across and saw Lenny controlling it with a small container on the floor and realised he was expecting to pour sweated onions into it.

A surge of blood pulsed through me. It was one of those moments. Although it felt like slow motion, it was too late to do anything – to even make a sound – before Lenny had tipped gallons of veal stock onto the kitchen floor. It was only for a second but, for this quantity, a second is enough time to pour what feels like an unholy flood gushing down the line of the kitchen and around the Crocs of most of the staff. Balls.

The German guard shrieked. 'Step away!'

A panicked baby-faced Lenny stepped back. 'I thought it was onion, Chef.'

'Get away, away from it!' she continued aggressively.

Shit, I felt guilty. I was somewhere else. I mean, he was an idiot for thinking it was going to go well, even if it was bloody onions. Why the fuck would you not look? But he was a sweet kid and I felt a tad protective. I turned away from my station as the tickets wound down and called for Toni, the Polish kitchen porter. He ran robotically, broom in hand, down the line of the kitchen, calling out 'Backs! Backs! Backs!' like the beeping noise of a reversing truck. He was a machine, sweeping enough of the gelatinous fat into the drains so that it at least wasn't a water feature any more.

'Sorry, sorry, sorry.' Lenny's mental circuits were being rewired with the spotlight of the kitchen eyes on him.

'You fool!' she continued. 'You'll be wiping this long after your shift.'

It was perhaps the worst thing to spill in a kitchen: stock in general, but specifically something as fatty as veal, which is a real endeavour to clean. It is for this exact reason that footwear is so important in kitchens. Crocs are open-heeled, so when something burning hot spills you can kick them off quickly, but they also used to be sealed without holes in them. I'd seen what happened to a chef when he turned the deep fryer latch off, spewing hot oil onto his hole-y Crocs. It didn't just burn his feet. It scalded his polyester socks into them.

I tried to soothe the situation from the grill, while not pissing off Leo, who was still focused in the heat of service and couldn't give two baby cow-turds for a teary commis.

'My bad, Chef,' I yelled over. 'Miscommunication. I'll sort it after service.' I then instructed Lenny to roll out some blue paper on the floor for some grip.

The German huffed and agreed. I could see Lenny was teary and lost for words. It was hard to watch that feeling of mass fuck-up. I saw it on poor Lenny. All you can do in these situations is tell a chef the truth, which is that tomorrow someone else spills the fat.

It was a long shift and the floor didn't quite feel the same for days. Sometimes, these cock-ups in kitchens rattle me all night, but I left feeling undistracted. I guess I just saw it differently that shift. Something went tits-up and it was okay. Better than, in fact.

A good shift turned into a better week. I called my sponsor and cracked on with Step 4. I found a new meeting and got a role as a greeter, which meant I had to show up there every week now. I connected with other newcomers. I picked up calls from addicts who wanted to check in. I wrote a gratitude list.

And then my old friend Adam called to serve one of those milestone slaps in recovery.

◆ ◆ ◆

Profound loss is full of contradictory emotions. Empty and full. Still and shaky. It's like you're in a furnace that's burning cold. I'd felt it before, but not while dry. This time, the only heat I could summon was anger.

It was inescapable just how much Jay's death stunned me. My bloodstream turned static and I couldn't tell if I was overheating or freezing – and frankly nor did I care.

Anger isn't a built-in, go-to emotion for me. I'm fairly passive. But it stormed inside me, almost out of a necessity to feel like I could do something – *anything* – to remedy or solve the loss, to control something irreversibly dealt.

As an active drunk, the solution was a lot more obvious. But now I was stuck.

A flurry of emotion and energy brewed inside with no outlet for release. I wanted someone to blame, to hold a culprit responsible. Jay was found cold in the early morning on the streets of Ladbroke Grove. Well, someone fucking knows – or was using with him and must have left him there. I know which dens are around there that he probably went to, the ones we used to live in. I started calling every den, every smoker, every dealer that we used to use with, even all the old numbers from the hotel – ones I was confident weren't dead, anyway. Those who I got through to, I would aggressively demand answers from when I didn't even really have a question. The anger trickled into hysterical tears in a first little wince of acceptance that my oldest pal was gone.

I read William Blake – one his mother chose – at his funeral. I hadn't seen her in years, since the days when we'd hide behind the sofa in the early mornings as the family got up for work. Seeing her again after all this time felt like walking into an old photograph that had stayed still without me. She was the same kind, steady woman, the sort who never gave up on her boy, no matter how rough the years got. And she was still holding up for her son now. I cooked a cut of beef for his family after and tried to stay busy, to not sit in the emotion that was trying to bubble up my throat.

My mind raced furiously: this can't be how it was meant to be? No, it's wrong. All wrong. Wrong body. Wrong funeral. Wrong fucking ending.

It didn't matter how I was leaping for an alternative. It was him. In a box. Dear sweet Jay. Gone. And there's no poetry in any of that. No meaning. No 'everything happens for a reason'; just the brutal arithmetic of it, the kind of hideously confusing maths that would make anyone grit their teeth and tear clumps of their hair out under whitened knuckles as they tried to make sense of it.

Life doesn't always come for the guilty, it comes for the exposed.

Life on life's terms.

16

Scallop tortellini with roe beurre blanc, caviar and crackling

Serves 4-6 Starters

Time 1.5-2 hours

Scallop Torrellini Roe Beurre Blanc

Sallop Moosse

150g Scallop, cleaned - muscle
70ml double cream
30ml creme fraich
Zest lemon
S & p

Magimix
Blitz until mousse

Paste Dough

250g 00 flour
2 large eggs
1 Yolk
pinch of Salt
Olive oil
Semolina

Blitz
Chill 30 mins
Knead 10 mins
Roll out

Roe Beurre Blanc

1 Shallot
300ml White wine
1tbsp White wine Vinegar
Scallop Roe - Cleaned from muscles
120gr Cold Butter
1 Clove garlic
Lemon

Reduce to 3/4 tblspn

To Finish

(depending on season)

Caviar Bulluga/Trout
Chives

Added pork option

- Fried Black pudding
- Pancetta
- Crispy parma ham
- Crackling

Pick up @ ocean catch from 4.00

'Oh, and there's just one more thing.'

I paused on the phone to a private client after finishing going through a detailed call for catering his five-course dinner party.

'The dessert, the tiramisu. I'd like it served on a body.'

I squinted into nothingness, my phone clutched to my ear as I tried to connect the dots. A body. A body of, like, a carcass? An animal? A body of water, perhaps?

'A naked body,' he clarified in a husky, erotic tone.

It was always something with this guy. The last time I served him an exotic meat menu – zebra tartare, alligator fillets, llama short ribs – I literally had to draw the line with his demand to go to the pet store.

A naked body – as in a woman, I assumed. Maybe not. Does he mean me? Why the fuck would he want me? Of course, he wants a busty blonde to make some loud joke and lick the plate clean.

My mind swarmed with logistics. You have to think differently when in a culinary state of mind. It's about thinking of answers to problems – solutions, not ethics – and quick. Surely there'd be a company that could help with this – someone who rented out naked people. Or was that just prostitutes? Maybe he meant a prostitute. I could go into a phone box and call one. I'd probably need to get them tested first. Dessert with a side of syphilis would be a new low.

I drew a line. 'No, I'm sorry. I can't help you there.'

'Oh, well. Can you bring some olive focaccia, then? My wife loved that.' Then he hung up.

Who knew? My mind had been exploring prostitution, unaware that bread was the other option. I hung up and looked to Karl, head chef from the Plum Gate, who was opposite me in my house.

'Did he want a prostitute?' he asked.

I nodded.

'Let's just do double focaccia.'

I was out of the restaurant and had become a private chef. Most remarkably, I was doing much of it with Karl. He also got sober shortly after me. As we struggled to live in the cogs of a commercial kitchen in sobriety, we started cooking together for clients, which I was more than happy to do. We had stayed close – he was only one of the few who did as he was someone who used a lot with me too. I think I was his canary in the coalmine. When I got admitted into treatment, he panicked and sought out something similar, like a man sprinting through the women and kids for the last lifeboat.

Karl had been bringing my kitchen skills up to speed under his fine, Michelin-ingrained standard. We spent months exploring flavours, dissecting every corner of the planet by spice and produce, and testing their dishes. We would fill time by getting close with our local mongers and butchery, getting our hands on whatever we could, and competing to see who could fillet bream closest to the bone and get the cleanest spatchcock from a poussin. It was a huge level up in sharpening the skills and culinary knowledge I had and needed. The best and worst thing about private cheffing was having more free time.

We were eerily shaky in a social sense and still learning about life while trying to now run a business. We have a lot of love for each other and still grate, resent and tussle day to day, despite a couple years of sobriety. But it's a show of just how long one is a newcomer in sobriety for – grown men not getting a hold on their insecurities for years.

We were lucky and got busy fairly quickly – or what we learnt was just the rush period of winter. Many private chefs make around a third of their annual earnings during November and December. It's where the pool of clientele suddenly burst open, a non-stop period of lavish spending by every tier: regulars, new spenders, corporate. That's something worth knowing by anyone who's thinking of fleeing the kitchen to go private. I was dumbfounded by my first private wage for the month of December. *New house? New car? I've made it.* But that was before the cold, humbling shock of the dead January-to-March graveyard.

After around a year of cooking together, Karl and I began graduating to bigger fish. What had been dinner parties and festive canapés moved on to foodies wanting culinary experiences and big events – and still the odd financier cokehead wanting zebra and hookers.

For anyone looking to enter the world of private dining, the kitchen can only teach you so much about some of the challenges that private cheffing poses. But I can divulge a few pearls of wisdom that working in this sector has provided:

1. The customer isn't always right. Trust your gut.
Money melts morals like goose fat on a grill. Separate what you feel you should do and what is right in your stomach. When rent depends on one event, you start convincing yourself that maybe tiramisu off someone's tits isn't such a bad fusion. It is.

Hold your ground. It's something worth thinking about on much simpler scales too. The same goes for cabaret waiters swinging plates of hot food on ropes, or any idea that starts with 'Wouldn't it be funny if . . . ?' Stick to your guns. It's worth remembering that your biggest source of new clientele is guests from your current clientele. Hold your standards. When it sounds like it'll go tits-over-pudding, it probably will.

2. You're responsible for the whole show, even when you're not. After a year of working bigger events we started getting sourced for the occasional household-name business. Some are gold, others surprisingly stingy. I catered the unveiling of Chanel's new autumn season. Fashion titans are a particular kind of client. It is, in many ways, like cooking for a toddler, for someone with more imagination than sense. They also look like they've crawled into their parents' oversized clothes. Factoring in health and safety requirements can be a task in itself, but ultimately the creativity begs a fun challenge. We went through weeks of menu development. They gave us their season's colour palette, with the wish for canapés to match but not clash with each other. *The Devil Wears Prada*'s Miranda Priestly would have a field day with my lack of descriptive vocabulary, but I saw purple, brown and beige.

Creatively, it was a fun test: beetroot *three ways* for the purple; a beet purée, served on a dehydrated slice of beet, garnished with pickled beet. Scallops with grated white truffle for the brown; and enoki mushrooms with miso mirin reduction for the beige. The food was a raging success, with slick-haired, hero-caped fashionistas coming to praise us below the decks.

They supplied the waiters – and the flared trousers with high heels they had to wear. These were ridiculous clothes for anyone. And it did lead to a clash of colours – three-way beetroot over their eggshell carpet.

It wasn't my waiter so it wasn't my problem. Except it was. Why? Because no one remembers whose fault it is; they just remember who fed them. The moral? You're the chef, but if the house burns down, even from someone else's match, it's more memorable than an astonishing canapé.

3. Treat home kitchens like bomb sites.
When you cook privately, some of the nicest homes in the world become your office. Think about who needs a private chef: mostly it's the top, top per cent. Although the kitchens of most clients are a sight to behold – and beautifully stocked with top-of-the-range equipment – they are almost always hugely impractical and fragile, whereas in commercial kitchens, all surfaces are predominantly stainless steel and are able to take heat, weight and general endurance. Most of these private kitchens are made of something like slapped Hungarian marble or flicked Ottoman vinyl, obscure-sounding materials that should be nowhere near service, and ones that could be ruined from the acidity of a single lemon wedge.

At one Knightsbridge townhouse, I left an S-shape stain on a marble counter from my damp blue roll that was nestled under my chopping board after slicing beef. When I tried to remove it, an outline was left, like the crime scene for a murdered Smurf. After my head waiter spent five hours scrubbing at it, it finally came off. Lesson learned: if in doubt, clingfilm the fuck out of everything. Just a touch of heat or acid on priest-tossed Bethlehem oak and it crumbles like stale Ryvita.

4. Overstaff.
I cooked for a wedding in Manchester; it was a big gig. Usually, people think cooking for weddings is the most stressful event possible: it is and it isn't. It's a lot of work, sure, but people

aren't actually coming for the food. Can you even remember what you ate at the last wedding you went to? It's far more stressful cooking an intimate multicourse experience for foodies who want something thought-provoking. But this wedding was somehow both. The groom was a real culinary mercenary and, for him, excitement-wise the food was on a par with marrying his squeeze. It was a whole new test, a logistical challenge: five courses for 150 people and a choice of duck or chateaubriand for main. And, being in Manchester, it was foreign territory when it came to butchers, mongers, utilities, the lot. And, of course, staff.

It seemed mad to bring staff from London, so I hired them from a local agency: eight chefs and ten waiters. All the chefs turned up, but only one waiter. Nine waiters were no-shows – an hour before serving. It was like a bad dream. We churned out all the plates, course by course, while simultaneously redressing the chefs as waiters in between to serve. Chefs look particularly different as you venture north. Seeing the girthy, Gallagher brother-haired Mancunian specimens, who were built like wardrobes, serve delicate seabass yuzu ceviche through their porky fingers, was like witnessing cows in a chicken coop, trying to blend in.

5. Beware of the middleman.

This is a crucial one. Often, you won't be directly dealing with the clients themselves. An assistant or housekeeper can be your point of call, so be sure to get on good terms with them. But also understand that, in almost all cases, they will put your head on the butcher's block to save their own. This also applies to everyone, whether the clients' own waiters telling you different timings or housekeepers offloading more jobs onto you. You're only hired by one client.

I cooked for a client a couple years back where the general

groundskeeper was my point of call. He was an older, East End man, cheeky and full of jokes that would always get a laugh exclusively from him. My job was to mostly prep multiple meals to leave in the fridge for the client to eat over a couple of days. After a fortnight or so, the groundskeeper would get me to prep extra after-dinner mini bites. He insisted on salted chocolate ones; 'Those are the ones she really loves.' I would, of course, make sure I had time to make these little baked sweets for post-dinner tea and coffee after I left.

As it turned out, the little wanker would just take them home for his afternoon tea. He laughed when I called out his chocolate-stained Tupperware. 'It's a compliment, mate. I love 'em.'

6. You're the expert. Push the dishes you're working on.
Some clients know what they want. Your job becomes a lot easier when you can push what you want to cook. Many clients actually want that, but just don't want to seem clueless. If you were going to a restaurant, wouldn't you eat what the chef recommends? Learn to be a bit of a salesman. Rib-eye? No, rare Scottish longhorn. Tuna? Bluefin Atlantic toro. Rocky road? Pebbled cul-de-sac. I worked in a kitchen that used to sell a dish garnished with high-altitude-aged parmesan flakes. Why? We kept them on the top shelf.

7. Get a driving licence.
This is perhaps an embarrassing one to say; it will seem like a real no-shit tip to many. I didn't have a licence until I was twenty-nine. And Karl didn't have one until he was even older. But thank god we didn't have them back in the day. I would crash into people on foot when I was pissed; a car would have been disastrous.

But not having one was a bad look, which Karl and I discovered when we were hired to cook a multi-course tasting menu for a couple of dozen connoisseurs in the Cotswolds. After a few lengthy Zoom meetings – detailing allergens, logistics and balancing flavours of depth in each bespoke dish – we ended with, 'Can someone give us a lift with the food?' The client couldn't quite believe it and labelled us as the nichest culinary company: stationary catering.

8. Don't shit where you cook.
Don't get over-familiar with clients. I have friends who have and it can get weird. There's often a point at these parties where things degenerate. Plates get licked clean, then coked up. And, of course, they want to offer the chef the chance to join them in their new dilated state. Often it's just an act from being high; they'd probably offer an SS soldier to come hash it out in that state. There's a good chance that they'll get hang-ziety the next day and you'll never hear from them again.

Also, don't shit where you cook in the literal sense. It would drive me insane how freely a chef would release his bowels in every house we got to at events. It's a hard one to fight. 'I need a shit,' he'd push back. 'What do you want me to do?' I don't want to impede his rights; he should be allowed. But also – yes, just bloody hold it in. The bathroom is the most popular place for people's noses at parties, so don't sully it.

9. Invest in yourself.
Get sturdy pans, durable aprons, functional equipment. Some people counsel against wasting money on knives. Well, I say get whatever makes you excited to use them. Create a workspace that makes things as smooth as possible. If you buy budget, you'll carry on buying budget until you don't. Don't wait for the lesson to hit you.

Get organised as best you can, or get a KP or chef you've hired to help on shift, especially when going mobile to events; you won't want to stick around once the job is done. I'll never forget the terror in my French kitchen porter's eyes in the rear mirror as I drove back to London from an event in Sheffield. We left too quickly. I piled him in the back seat along with pots, a fryer and ten loose cleavers. Every roundabout sounded like a steel orchestra, his eyes like two wide Parisian olives floating in terror.

Everything else you learn in the deep end. Private cheffing isn't a career; it's an endurance sport and it begs your best adaptation muscle. Everything predictive about kitchen life goes down the meat grinder. Each year has proved a new event, a new disaster, a new plate to spin while the old one wobbles.

But that's the beauty of it: adapting on the fly, managing chaos with a smile. The kitchens change, the clients evolve, the problems get weirder. Embrace it.

We didn't serve that tiramisu on a prostitute – just on plain old vanilla crockery. We packed up, wiped down and left just as their new, scantily clad friends arrived.

Then came the comedown, the lost bit after cooking. It hits you like the silence after service: the burners off, plates clean, adrenaline evaporating into the tiles and steel surface.

When you're sober, it's brutal. No drink, no high, nothing to celebrate with – just two chefs sitting on a sofa, staring at the wall with the kind of hollow achievement that echoes.

We'd cooked for the one per cent – creative, logistical masterpieces – but when it was over, there was only the void, the quiet spotlight of sobriety shining straight into your skull.

So we did what any high-functioning ex-junkies might: we played Tekken, broke the controllers and swiped dating apps like lab rats hitting a dopamine button that didn't work.

Karl tried to fill his hole more wholesomely; he decided he needed a dog – redemption through Labrador. He'd found an Italian rescue charity desperate for homes and sent videos of his flat, full walk-throughs like a proud estate agent. One night, the call came through.

'Mr Karl,' they said in apologetic Italian tones, 'after long deliberation, we conclude your flat and life is not up to standard for our rescue dogs.'

He froze. His jaw dropped. The man genuinely believed he was saving a dog and his soul. Then came the eruption.

'What do you mean a dog can't live here? A human lives here!'

It was a moment of pure operatic fury. The implication that his life was too depressing for a homeless, abused dog was devastating – and, if I'm honest, fucking hilarious.

We were finding our niche in dishes; pasta was becoming a big love. This was us coming into our tip number 6 ('push the dishes you're working on'). We loved doing it; food that excites the chef is almost always contagious to the customers too. And it's something for all budgets. Working with root veg purées garnished with everything from porcini or lobster tail to beluga or white truffle shavings, at its core pasta is something dear to all chefs, something we fall in and out of love with constantly.

Fresh pasta is the purest of tasks; deceptively simple, wildly unforgiving. There's no middle ground; it's either perfect or it's bin food. For us, tortellini became the muse. We had become clinical at rolling out doughy gold. Every chef has their religion when it comes to making pasta: some do the flour-and-yolk volcano, others the Magimix. Karl, trained under Pierre

Koffmann, swore by the latter. One egg to 100 grams of flour, a pinch of salt, a dash of oil and a spoon of yellow dye, which makes for the rich yolky illusion. I do like to add a tad more yolk with the illusion broken on me.

We were so confident in our pasta making that we tried to push it on pretty much every menu. That's the real challenge of private dining: adapting to every cuisine. Diwali parties, bar mitzvahs, kwanzaa . . . who the fuck could train in all that? By understanding the core spices of every region, we could translate our mostly French-European training, which was game-changing. For a dumpling-theme night, beurre blanc with Asian tones, with sake at the core instead of its usual dry Chablis. Doing this opened a rare space for culinary fusions that I'd not been concerned with in a commercial kitchen.

One time, we were prepping for a 100-person event, which meant 500 tortellini. I brought in two chefs, a KP and my now-teenage brother, Beetle.

Little Beetle – Isaac – wasn't so little any more. I was keen to make up for lost time. I'd been absent, shit and didn't know how to fix it. He wanted to be a chef, which was adorable and a tad terrifying, if only thinking of history repeating. But, then again, kitchens were never the problem. So I gave him a station. It turned out to be the best therapy I've ever had.

There's something profoundly human about pasta. It's surreptitiously tactile, meditative and grounding, an edible bubble of time to stand and stretch in for anyone who's ever lost their way. You knead, you roll and you decompress through a task that demands care but allows thought to drift. The best conversations I've ever had were over dough. I've also fallen in love, processed grief and healed kinship just from rolling egg and flour. There is no greater catalyst.

I showed Isaac the tricks: the kneading, the filling and my

highly inappropriate but effective technique of holding the steel sharpener between your legs, looping the tortellini round the 'metal cock' for the perfect fold of a tortellini vulva. He laughed so hard he nearly ruined the batch. We bonded, really bonded, over something we both connected with. The kid had focus, patience and finesse. He was a natural. Dad would have been proud. I know I was.

That night, it hit me: the fourth rule about private cheffing wasn't just about being well-staffed. It was about *who* you staff. Surround yourself with people you love, people who make the madness mean something. (Karl, for all his brilliance and unholy habit of taking catastrophic dumps in every bathroom he entered, was one of those people.)

It wasn't about the food, not really. It never is. It's about having something to care for that doesn't self-destruct when you touch it, about trying to put the world back together one plate at a time, even when you're cracked to fuck yourself. This whole recovery thing is just like it: simple in theory, brutal in practice. You may well ruin more batches than you get right and can fall out of practice so quickly. But when it comes out perfect – elastic, golden, alive – it explains why I fell into cooking, unwillingly. Just like one falls in love with anything.

17

Cherry frangipane tart

Cherry Frangipane Tart

30 cm Tart tin

Time / 1.5hr

Pastry — Pulse

250gr Plain White flour
150gr Butter, unsalted, cold
80gr icing Sugar
2 egg Yolks
pinch Maldon

Jam — Boil, Simmer, Stir, cool

day 2 In Advance

250gr Cherries, pitted
125gr Sugar
1 lemon
Splash water

To finish

Sugar Syrup (for glaze)
creme fraiche

Frangipane & filling

250gr Butter
250gr Caster Sugar
2 ~~3~~ eggs
250gr Almond – Blanched + Blitzed
70gr Polenta
2 vanilla pods
12 ripe cherries – half Slice – for decoration

For Seasonal Frangipane Tarts

Glazed Rhubarb

Peaches & maple Syrup

Strawberrie & marscapone

Burgundy poached Plums

Baked + fresh figs

- Fridge pastry – Grate onto Tart tin
- Bake tart – 160°C fan — 40 – 1 hour

A slice of Greggs pizza.
A tin of pineapple eaten straight, syrup and all.
A microwaved burger still sweating in its plastic.
A corner-shop cheese sandwich rammed with BBQ Pringles.
Cheerios drowned in orange juice . . .

Care to guess where we're headed? Felix Project donation bin roulette? Partridge in pear tree lyrics misremembered at speed? Or the final requests of America's most inwardly bred inmates?

Twenty-four stale chicken nuggets.
Cold Cumberland sausages from a breakfast shift two days ago.
One uncut cucumber dunked repeatedly into aioli (oddly suggestive).
A jar of cornichons topped with whisky.
A tub of Ben & Jerry's Phish Food ice cream, melted just enough to drink.
An entire Colin the Caterpillar cake.

It never fails to stun waiters, trainees or any civilian unfortunate enough to peer into a kitchen at staff meal-time. There's a whole book waiting to be written on what chefs eat. Because while we spend our days coaxing elegance out of butter and restraint, our own lunches often look like they were assembled during a blackout by a university student.

It's not that chefs don't eat well. They usually do – and constantly. Tasting richness all day is the punctuation of the shift: chasing balance, correcting seasoning, revisiting the same flavour until it's wrung dry. By the end of service, the last thing you want is another composed plate that your tongue has been coated with for hours. You want the culinary equivalent of static: sugar, salt, beige, meaningless. You want something alien enough to drown out finesse. Some chefs do take the piss, though.

It's the same reasoning behind that cliché of people who control boardrooms secretly craving chaos elsewhere. After hours of dominance, precision and posture, the soul wants something sloppy, humiliating and devoid of dignity. A dominatrix pissing on their fag burn in high stilettos – that's our Colin the Caterpillar cake.

Sometimes lunch isn't nourishment. It's decompression.

The real difference with private cheffing – building temporary kitchens and crews for events, pop-ups and one-offs, both obscene and intimate – is leftovers.

In a commercial kitchen, leftovers matter. It's all still active currency. Offcuts, veg stalks and bones remain gospel. There's pride in having kitchen knowledge to make a dish with trotters that's just as impressive as one made with the loin. It's the same style of menu, the same war; another chance to redeem yesterday's scraps and earn the full cash from the cow, bank from the piggy and gold from the goose.

Private dining doesn't have that luxury. There is no tomorrow of equal scale. No sequel. Just the wreckage of excess if they don't bring their appetite.

A staff meal, though? That can get fancier than a duchess in lace.

Not long after going solo, I cooked Thanksgiving for a prominent heiress. *Heir* and *ess* is the dream combo: people with money who actually want to use it, while women, broadly speaking, better understand how to treat catering staff like humans instead of rented furniture.

When I write menus, I offer a parallel path: normal luxury and unhinged. It's a polite way of asking, 'Are we behaving or are we slipping into something with the safety off?' She didn't hesitate.

Eight platters, each dish fully juiced. There was foie gras grated into the stuffing. Caviar, both Beluga and Osetra, and their own white albino Iranian, one for shellfish, one as garnish for the Russian salad, and one just open tableside for seasoning along with salt and pepper. But the best part was a separate, aggressive budget allocated purely to truffles: winter black Australians for the red cabbage, nitro-frozen Alba shaved with Perigord honey for the purée, and then the headline act: white Alba. The big boy.

My produce guy at this time had the second-biggest white truffle in the world. Allegedly. Now, who's to know how impressive that really is, like how your coke dealer says 'I've got one for £60 but this one for £100 that's a bit more . . .' Shut up, pack it up and take my money. He knew how to seduce. Truffles don't last long, so that noble title of second-biggest changes weekly. But it *was* huge and came with good enough marketing to hook me line and sinker. I'd seen smaller terriers. He was eager to give a discount and had me on sheer visuals.

I spent the full fungi budget and had assembled the world's most extravagantly aromatic spread of excess outside of Dubai.

The client, jetting off the next day, had no desire for leftovers. And, as per usual in those moments after serving, neither did I for the food I had been sautéing, reducing and seasoning for two days.

However, I did need to feed my staff of cooks – a couple of chefs. So I ordered pizza – two large margheritas, £25 each. I hadn't ordered Domino's in years and genuinely thought they'd made a mistake. Fifty quid for two pizzas. Daylight robbery – until we buried them.

We shaved close to a grand's worth of white truffle over steaming mozzarella and tomato sauce, a snowfall of flaky, erotic nonsense clinging to molten cheese, turning junk into something briefly transcendent.

We crouched in chefs' whites and ate the ludicrously indulgent fast food out of greased boxes with uncontrollable schoolboy grins. Who knew that fast food could be so show-stoppingly memorable? All you needed was hundreds of pounds.

I had to go to the South of France the next day, just outside Marseille. A couple of new clients I had acquired meant I'd begun spending more time around that area cooking for them. Serendipitously, it brought me to the one place I only ever wanted to cook in.

It's a remarkable feeling, travelling to cook – being needed and with someone willing to actually pay to fly me out, as opposed to paying for my Uber home. It hit differently, purpose validated with a boarding pass. That year, the destinations had begun to pick up. I'd been flown out to cook for someone at their Highland hunting lodge on the most secluded peninsular of the scattered Scottish Western Isles. It took planes, boats and rovers to get there, to the lodge on the rust-coloured hill roamed by stags with chests like busty Victorian harlots and shaggy ginger-haired cows chewing like apathetic teenagers. It was a secluded paradise in total isolation, a live-in postcard with no destination.

Produce had to be timed to one of two boat deliveries a week. Miss the boat and you'd be buggered. But venison? Venison was endless. Every cut, every shape – saddle, flank and chuck – was at my fingertips.

I'd go out with the gamekeeper on my time off. In one of life's better jokes, he was deathly allergic to meat thanks to a tick bite; a man who spent his days killing animals he couldn't eat, like something out of a cursed children's book; a butcher who lived on cucumber sandwiches.

I remember what struck me most on the hill was learning the seasonality of the deer. Half the season you shoot the hinds (females), the other half the stags (male). In stag season, the stags are nowhere to be seen – and vice versa, as you might imagine – so stalking them can take days that are fruitless. Mother Nature plays hard for you to get better than any.

But on the turnover day – literally the very day when stag shooting becomes illegal and passes over to the women and kids – the stags will suddenly appear and walk right up to the local houses and villages with the cocky assurance that their biological clock knows they're now untouchable. I mean, the confidence, the animalistic intuitive. How do they know something like that and pull through with it? Not the month or week even; the very day. I salute the boldness, the sheer swag in accepting these *Hunger Games* rules forced upon them and then flaunting their victorious vitality at the first opportunity. One year, they should swap the seasons around for a laugh.

Anyway, following that one-grand pizza, I landed in France with that rarest of luxuries: calm. It was almost unintuitive considering the work ahead, but remained a decompression that hit regardless, just from motion and purpose. Geography scratches a discomfort in me: movement without chaos, displacement with a pay cheque. I was locked into a job, which meant I was contained, safe. For a freelancer, that's as close as you get to sobriety by default and I was happy to avoid the meetings and schedule of an AA programme.

It at least lacked the worst vices of commercial kitchens: no money and infinite hours. I'd made the footballer's equivalent of moving from the Premier League to the Saudi League. Some of the glory and romance had evaporated, sure, but the wages were real, the schedule humane and it felt like you'd unearthed a secret loophole to the game that shouldn't be there.

The fear of the longer-term schedule, though, is constant. When's the next job? What if there isn't one? That quiet panic hums beneath everything – an occupational hangover from years of being chemically and existentially useless. No work lined up feels too much like relapse, as if you're standing barefoot at the edge of a cliff you've jumped off time and time again.

I arrived at the gated house, like every other time, down a remarkable pebbled drive through a lavender field. I was ushered in and welcomed by the housekeeper, the grinning but sharp-tongued Juliette. I settled my bags and went straight out to get produce. The tomatoes were in, and the cherries and apricots loomed supreme in their golden wicker baskets at the marché.

There's a sweet spot you can hit with familiar clients, usually around the third or fourth job. You become familiar enough with your surroundings to enjoy what you're doing on new levels, you know their palates, you know where you can buy produce and you can create menus with more freedom, with earnt trust.

I arrived on a Thursday, always a great day for fish there. It meant it was good to go heavier on the starter, a tartare, which is a relief for my prep. And, to finish, I usually start with a tart. I'm helping myself on another day by doing so. Starting a week's work with a naked fridge is nonstop for the first couple of days, but they get easier as you obtain more prep to store and use. There are not many desserts than can help on another dessert day, but when making a tart, I can make double the sweet pastry and store half for another dinner.

After day one – once you find your feet, re-vitalise the cupboards, ingrain the temp – there's a release, a quiet click. They know what you can do. And they like it. Even if you've cooked for them a dozen times before, there's always that moment where the shoulders drop. Trust is re-issued. Passport re-stamped.

If you're smart, you carve out the break. Discipline here isn't work; it's knowing when to take breaks. It's too easy to just keep going, because working alone with days in front of you, there's *mise en place* that's always continuous. But it's vital to stop for real time-outs if you want any focus left when it comes to serving.

A couple of days in, I forced myself to break after finishing serving lunch on the grand marble counter of the kitchen, ready to be taken out by the house staff to my client's pool side. Juliette, the seasoned kitchen helper, prodded me maternally as I left.

'Take, take, Ali. You need eat.'

She was right. I left the vast array of rich paella, carpaccio and slow-cooked brisket I'd been slaving over and wandered out onto a square of aggressively green well-kept lawn with my perfect sapid lunch – an overly buttered baguette with pickles in one hand and a dry roll-up in the other – and collapsed like a sniped animal. Thirty-degree Provençal sun worked its way into the oil slick of my forearms – garlic, butter, duck fat – baking that morning's service work deeper into my skin like marinade.

This was the life, right?

Of course it was. What else could anyone want? Flying in. Cooking alone. Best produce money can buy. No boss breathing down your neck. My menu. No rota. No future meetings. Paradise, by design. We fackin' did it, kid.

Was this the life?

Because before this – this alien second life – I'd always been an expert dodger of any responsibility: nothing to anchor me, no one dependable or to depend on. I'm clean now, but I've arranged my days with the same instincts: nomadic, single, unaccountable, useful only in bursts. And beyond the facade of appealing wonders, the meaning hasn't changed drastically. Service without consequence. Purpose on a hire basis. Alone.

I used to think loneliness meant having no mates. It took me years to realise you can be surrounded by people, clients, staff, diners and strangers, and still feel like the most isolated loner. Loneliness isn't silence. It's weightlessness. No pull. No one who'd really notice if you fucked off tomorrow. No one who needs you to show up when it's inconvenient.

That realisation landed right there, on the lawn with a mouthful of fatty baguette and the sun bleaching the sky white. Nothing was chasing me. Nothing was waiting. I had just a tart to attend to.

Frangipane is a classical favourite, the glue in your almond croissant, the baseline to marzipan. It's a nectareous paste that has earnt global hall-of-fame status, with most corners of the world having some equivalent. Equal parts almond, sugar and butter, the unholy trinity for calorie counters, you'd have to find a real stale wanker to protest against it. I add polenta for subtle grain bite, a little grit to the velvet.

It's not what the frangipane does that moves me. It's what it doesn't do. A sweet, nutty butter that acts as a vehicle for whatever you hang on it. It's a humble submissive team player, one that doesn't shout. It lets other bold, fleeting flavours have their moment – the ripe fruit of peak season, the kind of produce that only exists for a few weeks a year before disappearing again.

It's a funny relationship – chef to client, especially in a setting like this, one that's domesticated with vastly differing daily dishes. You're cooking food with layers of meaning and memory that the people eating it will never clock. And that's fine. That's the deal. They're buying dinner, while you're smuggling your personal archaeology onto the plate.

I've baked this almond tart in endless variations, almost always with a thought of someone else. There are flavours holding emotion, food that reminds me of time and personality. Figs always recall my dad, while peaches and maple syrup is all Jay and being young together. Anything syrupy, he holds really. With rhubarb, I can feel the cold shudder and detox of that Irish culinary school, while poached plums evoke Jason from rehab; he was eating them the first day we met. Strawberries are a classic; with crème fraîche, they make me think of my little sister Edi, back in London. She smothers her pancakes with them.

Cherries are a new one. In perfect bloom, they are little deep-rouge bombs of sweet and tart. In my French idyll, I cooked some down gently with sugar into a loose coulis, smeared them across the base of the pastry and then spooned the frangipane on top. The 'show' cherries I pitted, sliced and arranged in a neat circular descent, dipping them into the almond paste. Each press was final as the nutty quicksand instantly engulfed on impact. And into the oven.

It was a great marriage. Cherries already carry that faint nuttiness, like they've been flirting with almonds their whole life. The smell hit me halfway through baking and something clicked.

Juliette came in for her daily house duties and spotted the bake with her bloodhound nose for sugar.

'Backwell tart. Very good, British chef.'

Bakewell tart. Of course! I'd gone full circle – what a pretentious twat I am. For a moment, I guess I really thought I'd invented the most aggressively British dessert imaginable, the thing with synthetic icing you buy in plastic wrap on the way to school. That unmistakable aroma – almond, cherry, sugar – whether it's fresh or embalmed in cellophane is like a familiar tart of Christmas past. Everyone's already had a slice.

I was lethargic by the time dinner went out. No, more than that. I was flat.

Dinner was confit duck with potato terrine on celeriac purée – rich, fatty and unapologetically French. It was the kind of plate that leans back in its chair, unbuttons its briefs and lights a cigarillo without asking.

I plated long, careful slices of the tart – thin-tipped and cautious to not disturb the cherries. The smell of warm almond and sugar slowed everything down.

I thought of my mum and my siblings. I missed them in a way that felt stupidly primitive, like hunger or exhaustion, or like when your body clocks something essential is missing before your brain can label it. I hadn't seen them in months, not properly. The truth was that I hadn't really seen anyone. I'd just been . . . floating. I was existing like a chef between jobs: technically alive and vaguely functional, but isolatingly nomadic.

I'd forgotten how much of a little mummy's boy I was as a kid, the kind who'd tear up just from being away too long, like she was the only thing keeping the lights on. And she did, through everything. She stood there and watched me burn my life down in slow motion but still answered the phone like I was someone worth saving. The unfathomable turmoil we put our mothers through . . . like they signed up to be our sponsor, therapist and emergency contact for twenty years straight.

Then Dad. I miss Dad like an ingredient you only notice is absent once the sauce has already split, or like seasoning you forgot to add at the start and now it's all late. He didn't get to see any of this. He didn't get the reveal, how it worked out. He never saw me sober up for long enough to see it wasn't just a fluke, that I didn't just get clean but I stayed so for once. And he missed it. It's fucking classic of him.

And my head keeps moving like a prep list I can't finish: Jay, Jason, Teddy . . . People I love. People I lost. People I should've looked after. These are names that still sit in the back of my skull like old tickets stuck to the rail, orders you never got out, plates you never ran, calls you never returned.

'It's okay, Ali. They nearly done. Bedtime for you soon, 'Juliette chimed somewhat condescendingly in her rolling French accent as she scrubbed the greased serving platters and caught a glimpse of me deflating. I composed myself and smirked, knowing full well she hadn't had a good night's sleep in years, and wandered over to help her dry the platters. No decent chef goes early.

'I love this tart. It reminds me of my kids,' grinned Juliette in nostalgic awe.

The tart went out and plates came back obliterated; not politely finished, but chased. Fingers had dragged through the syrup and crumbs had been hoovered up like evidence. They thanked me. They always do and are great people. Alone again, with the oven ticking as it cools, it finally landed that I didn't escape isolation. I just learned how to plate it better. Distance isn't growth; it's misdirection, an overly bushy garnish. You can change countries, clients and kitchens, but still end up cooking the same ghosts on repeat. Memory travels faster than Ryanair; it's just as uncomfortable and doesn't give a feck about borders.

It wasn't dessert. It was a tart coming back to haunt me: familiar, comforting, faintly humiliating. It was sweet enough to disarm and, passed around with enough slices for all, still capable of undoing me with one mouthful.

I returned to my quarters, lost in thought. Does it matter, any of it? I can prep for chaos blindfolded. I'm not plating anything of sustenance. I remember a line that was said to me on my first week at rehabilitation that had made no sense to me:

We can only keep what we have by giving it away.

Perhaps my ending isn't a million miles from that of my uncle Nick who disappeared. What is it really worth, all this – to prep like a professional, unaccountable, and all to live like a greasy tart with no tomorrow?

18

Salted dark chocolate and ginger brownie with candied pecans and whipped cardamom mascarpone

Serves / 40 x 30 Baking tray

Time / 40 mins Total

Salted dark Choc Ginger Brownie cake Candied pecans, Cardamon Marscapone

Brownie

1. 250g butter
   600g dark chocolate → half 80% lint, half Bournville (300g / 300g) } Key for best coating
   80g peeled & diced ginger
2. 300g Sugar
   5 eggs
   Sea Salt

Candied pecans

100g caster sugar
2 tbsp water
200g pecans

Whipped marscapone

500g Marscapone — Beat solo first
2tbsp double cream
1tbsp icing sugar
1/2 tsp finely ground cardamom seed

☆ 20. min at 180°

I'm weary of anyone who enjoys birthdays. I can't stand them: summoning people you know and spotlighting – celebrating even – yourself. Through my teenage years, Dad used to say, 'Well done on making it this far.' I realise what he meant. I've got two of them now. There's the belly-button birthday (the regular one) and the other: the clean date. I just passed the latter last month. It's been five years since I used, five years since the morbid doctor told me I'd be dead by Christmas, five years since the thick-wristed Scottish matron, who looked like a cross between Susan Boyle and an overly ripe pear, hauled me into detox, like a wet carp into a net.

It has been taking over my head, particularly today, while making Milanese crab risotto and crème caramels for a client.

The risotto's a joy; I'm the bother. Some chefs think they're above it, but I don't mind the rhythm and attention it demands, nor the ache in your shoulder that it leaves behind. It's simple, yet easily noticeable from looks alone if it is made by someone who knows what they're doing or is bothered by making it. I pinch a fat wadge of saffron and watch the red threads dissolve into cream like tobacco in hot milk. The floral, earthy steam hits my face in a cloud of exotica. Then comes the flan: beige, wobbly and the spiritual dessert of seaside pensioners and post-op patients – crème caramel, the kind of pudding that tastes like it's already been eaten once before. They're just woke panna cottas really, lactose-liberal and non-offensive. Still, they make my client ecstatic and, today, that'll do.

Also on the list is dark chocolate brownie cakes. It's a signature recipe, one that's in the quadruple digits for the number of times it's been made. That Chinese proverb: 10,000 days to master the sword . . . well that's got to be close with this guy. I could get the texture right while blindfolded in a jail canteen during a prison riot. I'm making this batch a ginger number for a different kind of client.

I should be at an AA meeting. Every year I'm meant to go. Well, every week I'm meant to go, but announcing clean time every year – to get the polite applause, the hugs, the keyring – is vital. An addict's annual Hajj to Mecca. And yet, every year I struggle, I freeze. When they called for milestones the last time, I opened my mouth and nothing came out. The room waited. Seconds turned to hours. I sat there feeling like an imposter, as if someone would tap me on the shoulder at any moment, hand me a plate of gear and say, 'All right mate, nice try. Back you go,' before shoving it in my face like a custard pie in a Laurel and Hardy sketch.

I used to think recovery was about removing things. No drugs. No booze. No chaos. No silence. Gut your kitchen of allergens, sterilising before a service, and suddenly everything's calm, safe, professional. And you look the part: cleaner and sharper under a crisp, ironed-out apron.

That's not sobriety. Or, at least, it's not recovery. That happens after you've stopped actively setting yourself on fire when life starts handing you responsibilities like hot plates, one after the other, and you're expected to not drop them, but also embrace them.

It's not: 'Congratulations, here's a role on *MasterChef*, a restaurant and a book deal.'

It's more like: 'Twenty-three days clean. If I don't hear something good, I'm going to sniff my rent money and wander into traffic.'

That's how it starts. I was so fucked up when I came into recovery that it took me years just to unwind and say something with real, honest gravity. At some point, without noticing, I became someone's 'call', someone's 'if this goes wrong I'm fucking dead'.

I've got commitments, a sponsor, a circle to call, a couple of sponsees. Proper ones, too – men who shake like me, who try to fight feelings like sniffed-up bouncers outside Fabric. You tell them to ring you any time and they do in bursts of calls and silence – because we don't understand boundaries, either being welcomed within them or staying far away from them.

Nothing tests your serenity like the fryer smoking up and your phone buzzing with 'Mate, I'm outside my ex's house'. You don't get sober and become free; you get sober and become useful. And 'useful' goes hand in hand with 'responsible'. For any of us to have a fighting chance, we all are.

Even the meetings have changed. At the beginning, I went like a hostage, as if I was doing community service for crimes against myself and yet clinging to the seat with nowhere else to go, embracing Stockholm syndrome. Let me clarify: meetings didn't change, I did – slowly. And, over time, it stopped being about me.

And then cooking changed – or at least how I could use it. Then Christmas came, the first sober Christmas when I was convinced it was going to knock me. No work, no chaos, no distractions – just joy being shoved down your throat with tinsel and family. It's basically a tasting menu of testing emotions, course after course. But Christmas in addiction can sleigh a fine line of sentimental and triage. There are always people with nowhere to go, people who can't do Mum's roast because Mum hates them, or because Mum's house is danger, or Mum's using, or Mum's plain old dead. So I ended up cooking – big vats, big trays, like a kitchen in wartime. It was turkey for the lonely, stuffing for the trembling, gravy for the ones trying not to relapse in the bathroom. And, in the middle of it all, it hit me with weirdly nauseating sentiment: it feels better than getting high ever did.

Responsibility is what I'd been avoiding, but it was the final piece to change survival to a life worth living. It doesn't give you wind in your sails; it gives you the anchor.

These dates are stressful, the looming spotlight of recovery anniversaries. They're not celebrations. They're reminders – not of what you've achieved, but of what you are.

Still, I tie up the food boxes with rustic string and scrawl the client's name in my fanciest handwriting, like I'm the Duchess of Sussex running a deli pop-up for Netflix. The client is a musical legend and these are his weakness. I won't namedrop. I'll just deliver the bountiful selection with the all-important crème caramels, which I like to pun as 'Flan Zimmers', and head straight to my real appointment.

It's a small room in north London. I sit beside Maja, the girl I've been seeing for just five months. She squeezes my hand and smiles, the world sits still. It's profoundly disarming, as if Maja can see every ruined version of me at once and still doesn't flinch. The brownies are for her, packed with her craving for ginger.

I'm overcome with that feeling again. It feels like theft, like I've broken into someone else's life and decided to squat there. It has to be a glitch in some simulation. Or, maybe I did die that night. There was the blood, the blackout, the jeans around my ankles . . . perhaps this is just the weirdly wholesome afterlife I've been assigned. That might explain why Wendy, our midwife, is sitting opposite, dressed head-to-toe in full Nigerian regalia.

'So how are we feeling today?' Wendy asks, shuffling her papers with the professional optimism of someone who's seen things, but not quite my things.

'How are we feeling?'

Well, Wendy, this month marks half a decade since I stopped trying to die on purpose, five years since the morbid doctor, five years since I was dragged into treatment like a wounded spaniel. Five years ago, I couldn't feed myself without a bottle, lighter or spoon.

And now, apparently, I'm cleared to create life.

'We're doing just great! Big news, but we're fine,' Maja answers with her warm grin and those green eyes that could calm a stampede. She has a way with people. If *I* said that, it would sound unconvincing, enough to start a panicked stampede.

'Yes . . . I see you're not married.'

The tone is politely judgemental in the exact register my grandmother would have applauded. We aren't even living together, Wendy. Please pace yourself.

'Well,' she continues, softening, 'this is a blessing. And, trust me, there's no situation I haven't seen before.'

She launches into trimesters, vitamins and breathing patterns, warning us that it's long, mostly for 'Mummy', who should get to the bottom of the migraines she's been having. Then Wendy begins the world's most glacial Q&A in order to fill out a form. I try to focus at first: name, address, all the beginner questions. But somewhere around 'iron levels', my brain floats away, drifting toward an ultrasound photo on her desk – a grainy blob of static, like a soufflé collapsing in slow motion.

That's what's happening now. A soufflé kid. My soufflé kid. Fuck.

'And this one's for Dad,' Wendy snaps me back, with her stern Nigerian teacher-voice.

Maja looks at me like a parent at a nativity play whose child has forgotten his only line.

'Sorry, what was the question?' I lean forward, keen to pretend I haven't mentally vacated my own skull.

'Any history of substance abuse? From Mum or Dad?'

Her finger hovers expectantly over the form.

'Ah, well. Yes.'

The hovering finger retracts. Eyes widen.

'Yes, what?'

'Yes as in . . . tick. Next?' I offer, hoping this is a multiple-choice job.

'What substances did you have a problem with, Mr Gill?'

Surely we're not doing this – not again. Five years later and I'm still reading out the world's saddest wine list. Usually 'I'm an addict' is enough to shut down the nosiest of nosy people. Not Wendy.

We go through the classics.

'Marijuana?' Yes.

'Cocaine?' Yes.

'Amphetamine?' Sure.

'Heroin?' Yep.

'Oh dear!' she blurts, then immediately apologises for her humanity leaking out.

'Ketamine?' Yes.

'Mephedrone?' No.

She beams like I've just won a spelling bee contest.

'Solvents?'

'. . . big time.'

She deflates again.

By the time we finish, I'm basically reading out my own war crimes at a tribunal. I glance at Maja apologetically, but she's already choking back laughter, her pity wrestling her hilarity to the ground. Wendy, meanwhile, has the expression of someone completing an incident report beyond anything she's ever ticked before.

I try to assure her.

'I don't do anything now. I'm in a programme. Clean for years.'

'Okay . . .' she types, both baffled and worried, 'so I will write, "He abused them all a lot but, he's VERY sober now!"'

Fair.

'And for Mum?'

'Nope.'

A clean slate. Not even a whiff of Tippex. Granny would be thrilled.

Wendy composes herself, reads through the notes, then looks up with a diplomatic smile.

'You're a healthy, low-risk couple overall . . . but there is one part of the form that has tipped your combined mental-health score into the red zone.'

'Was it her migraines?' I venture hopefully.

Maja shakes her head, smirking already.

'No, I'm afraid it's . . . all your naughty abuse, Mr Gill.'

She winces as she says it, like an Irish nun being forced to talk about sex education.

'Because you score as a couple, Maja will need to attend extra appointments for her mental wellbeing.'

'Perfect,' Maja says, as her grin suddenly vanishes.

I laugh awkwardly. Inside, I feel an odd familiar punch, the guilt of my past reaching its long fingers into someone else's future. Even now, even here, I'm creating extra admin.

We stand to leave, hands tight together, a united front against past bureaucracy.

'Oh, Mr Gill?' Wendy calls as I'm pulling on my jacket.

I turn.

'On your five years last month – well done.'

And, for the first time all day, it hit.

Outside, the north London air strikes us and Maja slips her arm through mine. The street noise softens, as if someone's turned the city down a notch to let me hear myself think.

Five years.

Wendy's congratulations shouldn't have meant anything; it was practically an administrative courtesy, the kind of line they probably teach on page one of midwife school. But it hit somewhere old, somewhere soft – the place Dad used to pat when he'd mutter, 'Well done on making it this far', in that half-distracted way that somehow meant everything.

I hadn't realised how badly I needed someone to acknowledge I'd made it this far in order to trigger some self-recognition that I hadn't slid back down the slope, that I was still here, upright, unpoisoned.

I've spent years waiting for the other knife to drop, waiting for someone to yank my apron off and tell me I've overstayed my welcome.

Five years ago, I couldn't make a croque madame without chemical assistance. I couldn't wake up without negotiating with my body. I couldn't look in a mirror unless I was already numb. I was a chef who couldn't feed himself – a profoundly sad kind of irony.

And now I'm walking out of a maternity clinic. What if the baby is like me, and like the dad before me, and we'll go through it all again: that panic on watching him breathe, then the panic of him watching me breathe.

It doesn't seem right: a man who used to treat his life like an off-cut of bad meat is to be responsible for another actual human? Who voted for that? Sobriety has proven to be the most surreal kitchen apprenticeship. Although it's been five years, it feels like I just got on the larder section and I'm being sent to lead the pass.

Getting here hasn't exactly been a glam makeover montage worthy of this conclusion. A lot of it is just repetitive, boring, painful and humiliating. It's *mise en place* every day: the same knife kit, the same station, the same discipline. And if you slack off, chaos doesn't just creep in. It kicks the door down and starts throwing pans.

◆ ◆ ◆

I look at Maja. She smiles back, muting the inner storm battering my head into instant static, that same look that undoes me every time – the one that says she sees the colossal wreckage, the resurrection and the ridiculousness – and yet somehow doesn't run as fast as she can. In just that moment itself is that life I was once told about, the one beyond my wildest dreams. If there's any proof that trading in an empty bottle and a hangover was in exchange for the keys to the kingdom, this is it.

'Five years,' she whispers.

I nod. 'Yeah.'

For the first time, this anniversary doesn't feel like I'm getting away from something. I'm not counting days, nor desperately running for space between now and then. *Mise en place* is done and the pass is lighting up for something new.

Not a countdown. A beginning.

Recipes

Drunk beef with whipped Roquefort and port reduction

Ingredients

500g beef fillet, trimmed
½ bottle of port
2 bay leaves
Thyme sprigs/bouquet garni
Dehydrated baguette slices/wonton spoons for serving
2 tablespoons caster sugar
Neutral oil (for searing)
Shallot to serve (finely brunoised)
Chives (finely sliced)

For the dressing:
100g mascarpone
150g Roquefort cheese
50ml double cream
Pinch of salt

Method

1. Marinate overnight. Put cut of trimmed fillet in a container and pour the port until fully submerged. Add hard herbs – 2 bay leaves and a couple sprigs of thyme. Seal well and leave in the fridge for 4 hours. If using dehydrated baguette

slices, slice thin as possible and put in the oven at around 100°C for a few hours until dry enough to snap.

2. On to the whipped Roquefort. Whisk the mascarpone on its own first, then add the Roquefort slowly – of all the things you can split, blue cheese is particularly worth avoiding. Keep whisking and add a pinch of salt and a dash of double cream to loosen. Don't over-whip – the texture should be just stiff enough to pipe. Fridge to chill.
3. Port reduction. Take the fillet out of the port and discard the hard herbs. The cut should have a deep rouge colouring. Pat it dry with a jay cloth and paper towels, then leave to sit in a dry container in the fridge uncovered for a further hour. Meanwhile, put the port that's been bathing your fillet into a saucepan and on the boil. Reduce with the sugar, until thick and syrupy and it emits slow, lava-like bubbles.
4. Sear and slice. Sear the fillet on a piping-hot skillet with a tsp of oil for about 10 seconds on each side. Then rest further for 45 minutes in the freezer to firm up for easier cuts. Slice as thinly as possible – long smooth cuts.
5. Assemble canapé. Place a long slice of drunk fillet on a slice of dehydrated baguette (anything but flat). Pinch it up so it sits with a woven groove, then pipe or spoon a dollop of whipped Roquefort in the raised crevice. Drizzle the cooled reduction down the side of the creamed cheese. Garnish with the finely sliced chives and shallot.

Crab linguine with chilli, fennel and lemon

Ingredients

1 tbsp fennel seeds
2 small red chillis, deseeded and diced
2 cloves garlic
Olive oil
150g brown crab meat
300g white crab meat
2 tbsp crème fraîche
2 large unwaxed lemons (zest and juice and to serve)
500g linguine
Maldon salt
1 generous handful mixed of parsley and chervil picked and roughly chopped
Black pepper
Fennel fronds for garnish
Optional claw/shell for decor

Method

1. Toast the fennel seeds in a dry pan for 30 seconds until smoky, being careful not to brown. Crush in pestle and mortar. Add chilli and garlic, and grind into a rough paste.
2. Heat 2–3 tbsp of olive oil in a wide pan. Add the paste and

cook on medium-low for 3–4 minutes to soften. No colour.

3. Add brown crab first and stir into the oil until it melts in. Then build and season. Add zest with juice of 1 lemon, fold in crème fraîche and finally white crab. Keep the heat low – you're just warming through, not cooking the crab further. Take it off the heat if it starts bubbling.
4. Cook linguine in boiling salted water until al dente. Drain, saving ½ cup pasta water.
5. Add linguine into the crab pan. Toss on low heat and add pasta water, a splash at a time, to loosen and gloss. Season with Maldon salt and black pepper. Fold through parsley last.
6. Plate up and finish with a generous drizzle of quality peppery virgin olive oil, fennel fronds and extra lemon zest. Lemon wedge on the side. Claw/shell for theatre. Serve immediately.

Junkie fried chicken

Ingredients

1kg large chicken thighs and drumsticks
Neutral oil for frying

Brine:
1 litre whole milk
50g salt
30g sugar
1 tbsp black pepper
2 bay leaves

Dry mix:
500g flour
100g corn starch
2 tbsp fine white and black pepper
1 tbsp salt
1 tbsp onion powder
1 tbsp garlic powder
1 tbsp dried oregano
½ tbsp paprika
½ tbsp ground cumin
½ tbsp cayenne pepper
½ tbsp chilli powder (optional)

Wet mix:
3 eggs
300ml full-fat milk

Method

1. Lightly pierce the chicken with a sharp knife to brine for 3 hours or overnight. I use whole milk with bay leaves, salt, sugar and peppercorns, but buttermilk/sour cream/yogurt/water works in the brining process if preferred. Heat the mixture on a medium heat until the salt and sugar have dissolved. Only once fully cooled should you add the chicken for the brining process. If you've ever wondered why some poultry has somehow been elevated into a new dimension, it's because it's brined. But if you feel brine is long and life is short, you can skip to step 2, or even step 3.
2. Once brined, remove the chicken and lightly pat dry. Place into sealed bags to sous vide at 70°C in a gastro container for around 4 hours until cooked and tender. Leave to fully cool; the batter won't stick if it's still emitting steam. (Cold chicken makes for better batter. If you have time, put it in the fridge uncovered to cool further for 30 minutes.)
3. Set up your dunking stations. Combine your dry mix thoroughly in one tray and whisk your wet mix in the other. Heat your oil ready for frying in a deep fryer or sturdy cast-iron pot. Aim for around 170–175°C. (If you don't have a thermometer, a small pinch of flour in the oil should fizz instantly and rise.)
4. Dunk your cooled chicken pieces into the dry mix, shaking off any excess rub, then submerge into the wet mix, repeating the process a couple of times. Press the flour on firmly for craggier bits, then let the chicken sit on a rack

for 5–10 minutes before frying so that the coating hydrates and locks on.

5. Fry until the batter is a golden-brown crisp. Keep the oil temperature between 165 and 175°C, and don't overcrowd the pot. As a rough guide, do so for 6–10 minutes, depending on size, but remember that, since the chicken is already cooked, you're frying purely for crust. Drain on a rack (not paper) and season with a pinch of salt.

Braised octopus with tomato, Chablis and a sweet miso purée

Ingredients

1 whole octopus, defrosted from frozen and beak removed
Olive oil
1 fennel bulb
3 large shallots
3 cloves garlic
1 tbsp tomato purée
½ tsp smoked paprika (pimentón)
⅓ bottle Chablis/dry, acidic white wine
2 tins canned tomatoes or passata
2 tbsp dark soy sauce
1 bay leaf
1 tbsp capers (or a splash of caper brine)
Salt and pepper
Gastrique to finish seasoning
Tarragon and lemon for garnish

For the purée:
2 large sweet potatoes, peeled and cubed
2 tsp red miso
150ml melted unsalted butter
Pinch of salt
Splash of whole milk to loosen

Method

1. Prepare a pot/Dutch oven big enough to fit the limp octopus. Slice fennel and shallots, and sweat over a medium heat with a dash of oil. Microplane in garlic and add tomato purée and smoked paprika. Cook for a couple of minutes until softened and fragrant, then remove from pan and set aside.
2. Add white wine to deglaze and let it bubble for a minute. Add canned tomatoes/passata, soy sauce, bay leaf and a splash of water if needed. Lower your octopus in – it should be mostly submerged (but doesn't have to be totally invisible). Turn heat down: a slow bubble emerging every other second is ideal. Cover and leave for about 1½ hours until tender. (Service-proof cue: the knife should slide into the thick part of tentacle with little resistance. If it's still chewy, it just needs time, not more heat.)
3. While the octopus cooks, boil the sweet potato until fully soft. Leave to sit for a minute to lose some liquid before blending with melted butter, miso and salt in a bullet blender until silky smooth. At this point, adding a splash of double cream to loosen is optional. The purée wants to be silky and velvet, not stiff mash.
4. Once the octopus is cooked and tender, remove and place on a tray to rest. Pass the tomato sauce through a fine sieve, return it to the pot and reduce on a high heat, stirring often so it doesn't burn. Add capers (or caper brine) at the end. Taste and season (gastrique to finish if needed). You want it thick enough to coat the back of a spoon and fall off slowly, so not watery.
5. Slice each tentacle off and fry with a dash of oil on medium-high heat until crispy outside. Dry the tentacles first with kitchen roll as this will make them crispier.

Don't overcrowd the pan. Let it sit and colour before tossing.

6. Serve each tentacle over a smear of sweet miso purée, drizzle it with the reduction and finish with a lemon wedge and fresh herbs – tarragon lends itself perfectly. Enough lemon is important and think about your other acids (gastrique and tomato reduction) to balance your rich octopus and buttery purée.

Wood pigeon salad with chanterelles and a walnut dressing

INGREDIENTS

For the mushrooms:

100g chanterelles (use local – morels and chestnuts always work)
Splash of oil/small knob butter (for sautéing)
½ garlic clove, grated
1 tsp dried thyme and sage
Salt
Pepper

For the pigeon:

2 pigeon breasts
Salt
Black pepper
Splash of oil
Butter for basting
1 bunch rosemary (for basting)
1 sprig thyme
1 garlic clove, crushed

For the walnut dressing:

1 tsp Dijon mustard
1 tsp honey
½ clove garlic (grated)

1 tbsp sherry vinegar
1 tbsp walnut oil
1 tbsp olive oil
1 lemon, juiced
Salt
Pepper

For the salad:
2 large handfuls watercress
Handful of pickled blackberries
2 tbsp pine nuts, toasted

Method

1. In an oiled pan, add your cleaned mushrooms over a medium-high heat. Let them take colour – real colour. Don't stir for the first minute; let them catch. Once browned, add grated garlic, dried thyme, sage and a decent knob of butter to let them baste and shine. Season and set aside at room temperature. (If they start sweating water, you've overcrowded the pan or it's not hot enough.)
2. For the pigeon breasts, season generously with salt and pepper. Be sure they've spent enough time out of the fridge to get close to room temperature (cold pigeon tightens and cooks unevenly). Heat a pan over medium-high heat, add a dash of oil, then place pigeon breasts skin-side down and press downward with fingers. Cook for about 2 minutes per side – the pigeon should remain pink and tender inside. Add butter, thyme, rosemary and crushed garlic. Tilt the pan and baste with a spoon like you mean it. Remove and rest for 5 minutes before slicing. (Service-proof cue: it should feel springy not

firm. If it's grey inside, you've gone too far. Resting is non-negotiable.)

3. Make the walnut dressing. Start with the Dijon mustard in a mixing bowl and whisk together vinegar, honey, microplaned garlic and seasoning. Add walnut oil, along with olive oil bit by bit, whisking until emulsified. Taste and adjust for sharpness or sweetness using salt, pepper and lemon juice. (If it splits, re-whisk with a touch more Dijon or a drop of warm water.)
4. Time to assemble the salad. Lightly dress the watercress and place onto serving plates. Don't drown it as watercress collapses fast. Dress in a bowl then plate. Spoon it over warm mushrooms and arrange blackberries. Slice the rested pigeon and then plate (it should be warm).
5. Finish by spooning more walnut dressing over the pigeon and scatter toasted pine nuts. Serve immediately.

Tagine à la Skippy

Ingredients

Salt
2 large shallots, diced
Olive oil
1 tsp tomato concentrate
1kg mixed veg
Potatoes (Maris Piper/King Edward) peeled and chopped
Sweet potato, peeled and chopped
Carrot, peeled and chopped
Aubergine, chopped
Pumpkin, peeled and chopped
Courgette, chopped
5 cloves garlic, peeled, minced
2 tsp ras el hanout
1 tsp ginger, peeled and minced
½ tsp ground coriander
½ tsp cumin
1 tin tomato or passata
400g cooked chickpeas
300ml vegetable stock
Pinch of saffron
1 tbsp harissa paste
200g yogurt

Parsley
Peanut butter
Soy sauce
3 limes (zest and juice)

METHOD

1. In a large pot or Dutch oven, salt and sweat the shallots down with a dash of oil over medium heat until softened. Add the tomato concentrate and stir.
2. Take a quarter of your veg and cut them down – in half roughly – then toss them onto a lined baking tray. Season with an extra tablespoon of ras el hanout, a pinch of salt and a drizzle of oil. Toss like you mean it then set aside and leave them be. They're for the finishing flourish.
3. Add the garlic, the remaining chopped veg and spices to the softening shallots. Cook for 10 minutes on a medium-high heat, tossing regularly. (Let it catch a bit on the bottom; that adds flavour.)
4. Add the tomatoes, stock, drained chickpeas and saffron, and season with salt. Keep the heat on high for another 10 minutes to get it moving. Reduce the heat, cover and simmer for around 30 minutes, stirring occasionally until the veg is soft. (Service-proof cue: the potatoes should crush easily with a spoon, while the sauce should be thick enough to coat.)
5. Fire up the grill to max. Slide your reserved tray from earlier under for 5–10 minutes until nicely charred. (Keep an eye on it; it should be charred, not cremated.)
6. In a mixing bowl, mix the harissa paste into the yogurt with salt and a lime (using some of the zest and the juice).

7. Once the veg is just soft to a knife's touch, it's time to add your 2 tablespoons of peanut butter, 2 limes (zest and juice) and a teaspoon of soy sauce. Blitz in a food processor or hand blender. Smooth but doesn't have to be velvet – more rustic than elegant.
8. To plate, ladle into bowls and crown with charred veggies and chickpeas. Layer the torn parsley with the grated lime zest and dot with the harissa yogurt. Serve hot.

Fig and taleggio tart

Ingredients

100g butter
2 shallots
Dash of red wine
1 tbsp demerara sugar
4 large eggs
200ml double cream
Salt
5 squared sheets of filo pastry
8 figs, sliced or quartered
200g taleggio
Bunch of thyme sprigs
Chives to garnish

Method

1. Preheat the oven to 180°C and start with the shallot jam. Slice the shallots finely and cook down slowly with half of the butter, tossing to cover and leaving to sweat over a low heat. Once soft and glossy, turn the heat up and add a dash of red wine and the sugar. Let it bubble hard for a minute to cook off the booze and then drop back down to a lazy simmer until it turns into a dark sticky jam.

2. Whisk the eggs and cream together in a mixing bowl. Season with a generous pinch of salt.
3. Melt the remaining butter in a pan or microwave and have it ready in a bowl with a brush. Grease the parchment paper, then line a 10-inch tart tin and begin layering the filo, brushing each layer with melted butter as you do so. Don't stress about pastry hanging off; just cut this with scissors once you're done. (If you're lagging and the filo starts drying out, cover it with a slightly damp tea towel.)
4. Scatter half of the shallot jam around the base of the tart and layer the figs. Pour in the egg mix until just 2cm from the top rim, add small chunks of taleggio and the rest of the jam on top. Sprinkle a pinch of salt and add lightly oiled thyme sprigs.
5. Put the tart in the oven for about 30 minutes until the pastry is golden and the tart is set (the centre should be soft but not wobbly). Rest for 10 minutes before slicing. Finish with fresh herbs.

Truffled egg toast

INGREDIENTS

3cm-thick slice of square white bread
150g fontina cheese, grated
2 free-range egg yolks
1 tsp truffle oil
Sea salt flakes and freshly ground black pepper

METHOD

1. Preheat the oven to 180°C/Gas 4.
2. Lightly toast the bread on both sides and place it on a baking sheet. With a very sharp knife, cut a shallow square well (about 5cm) into the centre of the bread. Cut the outline and press down the bread within the cut lines to create the well.
3. Distribute the grated fontina evenly around the well and pour the egg yolks into the centre. Place the baking sheet into the oven and toast for about 3 minutes until the cheese melts (the yolks should still be runny).
4. Take out the toast, stir the runny yolks slightly, dribble truffle oil over the surface and season with salt and pepper. Eat immediately.

Ketty tuna (Eastern niçoise salad)

Ingredients

For the tuna:

400g sushi-grade tuna loin
Neutral oil (rapeseed/rice bran)
Sea salt
Fresh cracked black pepper

For the potato seasoning:

1 tsp togarashi (or chilli flakes)
1 tsp sesame seeds
A pinch of nori flakes/crushed dried seaweed

For the salad:

150g new potatoes
Neutral oil (for potatoes)
Salt and pepper
100g samphire, blanched
8–10 cherry tomatoes, halved
1 small cucumber, sliced and pickled
5 bulbous radishes
Handful of mixed leaves (frisée and shiso)
2 soft-boiled eggs (jammy, not chalky)

1 ripe avocado, whizzed into purée (loosen with lime, yuzu and sesame oil)
Black sesame seeds (for purée finish)

For the yuzu dressing:
2 anchovy fillets (minced to paste)
½ garlic clove, minced finely
1 lime (zest and juice)
2 tbsp yuzu juice
½ tsp wasabi paste
1 tsp honey
1 tsp mirin
2 tbsp light soy sauce
1 tsp sesame oil
Optional heat: pinch of chilli flakes or chilli oil

Method

1. Crank your oven to full grill. While that's heating up, boil potatoes in aggressively salted water until just tender (knife in, no resistance or collapse). Drain and let them steam dry until the surfaces look chalky. Keep the boiling water and put in your eggs for 7 minutes for a soft boil.
2. Once the potatoes are cool enough to handle, lay them on a tray and crush gently with the curve of a ladle. You want them flattened but still clinging together. Coat with a neutral oil, season hard with salt, pepper and a good pinch of the potato seasoning. Toss like you mean it, then slide under the grill for 8–12 minutes until edges are charred. Set aside to cool.
3. Tuna. Get that guy trimmed and sliced. This dish improves with scale: longer loins give you clean, elegant slices later.

Heat a dash of cooking oil in a pan on the hottest setting. Press each side for around 10 seconds until coloured. You're just searing for a beige seal and core raw.

4. Dressing. Put the anchovies, miso and garlic into a bowl and mash to a paste. Whisk in the rest. Add liquid or miso to make sure it's not too thick or too runny. The texture should sit somewhere between runny honey and thick syrup; it should coat, not drown. Season properly. Taste again (always again). Find the spot where salty and sweet battle sour.
5. Sharpen your longest, most trusted knife. Dry the blade. Dry the tuna. Dry everything. Slice into thick, confident portions of about half an inch. This isn't carpaccio; it's more delicate flesh. Fan slices into a loose arc on the plate so that they overlap like a hand of playing cards.
6. Dress the washed leaves with yuzu dressing and place centre plate. Add the accoutrements accordingly: crushed potatoes, samphire, pickled cucumber, radishes and tomato. Finish with the soft boiled egg in half, the two halves overlapping each other and the golden, perfect yolk on show. Season. Garnish with coriander and a fresh shiso leaf. Decorate rim with squirts of avocado purée topped with black sesame seeds.

Pork belly with miso maple reduction and celeriac remoulade

Ingredients

For the braising:

2–3kg pork belly, bone in, skin scored
3 tbsp red miso paste mixed into 1 litre warm water
250ml white wine
250ml chicken stock
Sea salt

For the reduction:

2 medium shallots, chopped
1 tsp oil
300ml miso pork broth
200ml red wine
1 tsp white wine vinegar
Small bunch thyme, tied
2 tbsp Dijon mustard
1–2 tbsp maple syrup
1 tsp miso paste

For the remoulade:

1 egg yolk
2–3 tsp wholegrain mustard

1 clove garlic, finely grated
100ml olive oil
200ml flavourless oil (veg/sunflower/rapeseed etc.)
½ large lemon (juice and zest)
Salt and pepper
1 celeriac
Chives, finely cut
Apple julienne (for seasoning)

Method

For the pork:

1. Heat the oven to 120°C. Place the pork belly into a deep baking tray and submerge in hot braising liquid (miso water, white wine, chicken stock, salt). Add more liquid if needed to cover. Seal thoroughly (parchment first, then foil and lid). Braise for 5 hours until tender.
2. Leave the pork to rest out of liquid. Once cool, you should be able to slide out the bones with ease. Remove the skin (it should peel straight off). Wrap the belly meat in a container and put it in the fridge until serving.
3. Place the skin on a lined tray and carefully scrape off any excess fat as best you can. Then put it back into oven by itself at 90°C to dry out for a few hours. You want to really dry it out from some of the fat and braising liquid. The aim is basically to make a dehydrated cracker to crisp up like pork scratching. This is the key to sublime pork skin; it lets it crisp while maintaining flavour when you fry.
4. Once dried out, cut the skin into rectangular portion shapes and fry in a deep fryer or deep cast-iron pan until puffed and crisp. Don't do it all at once. Drain and season with salt straight away.

5. To serve, reheat the belly in a medium oven until hot through, top with crispy skin and serve with drizzle of reduction and a side of remoulade.

For the reduction:

1. Heat 1 tsp oil in a pot and sweat the shallot until soft.
2. Turn the heat up high and add the red wine first, let it cook for a moment, then add the pork broth, vinegar, thyme, Dijon mustard, maple and miso. Bubble on a medium heat for about 10 minutes, then strain through a fine sieve. Season as you go, but take note that it will intensify as it reduces – particularly salt from miso.
3. Return the smooth mix to the stove and reduce to a thick jus. Finish with a hand blender for ultimate rich silky texture.

For the remoulade:

1. The remoulade base should be like a thick mayonnaise. Start with the egg yolk and wholegrain mustard in a mixing bowl and whisk. Add the oils slowly in a thin stream so it doesn't split. Add the garlic, lemon juice and zest, then season with salt and pepper to emulsify.
2. Peel the celeriac and finely slice on a mandolin, then cut into fine julienne matchsticks. Fold through the emulsion.
3. Finish with the chives, apple matchsticks and a drizzle of olive oil.

Soda bread

Ingredients

300g wholemeal bread flour
200g plain flour
1 tbsp bicarb, sieved
Big pinch of sea salt
2 generous tbsp black treacle
250ml unsweetened kefir
250ml Guinness

Method

1. Preheat oven to 200°C and have your standard 9-inch (23x13cm) loaf tin on standby (or two smaller tins if preferred).
2. In a large mixing bowl, combine the wholemeal flour, plain flour, bicarb and salt. Mix well so it's evenly distributed.
3. Make a well in the centre and pour in the treacle, kefir and Guinness. Stir together, then work with your hands until fully combined. The dough should be wet, sticky and porridge-like (not a kneadable dough).
4. Pour into the prepared loaf tin(s) and smooth the top. Bake for 45 minutes, lowering oven to 180°C after 10 minutes.

5. Remove the loaf from the tin and return it directly to the oven rack for a final 5 minutes. It's done when it sounds hollow if tapped underneath.
6. Cool on a wire rack, slice in and butter up.

Chicken liver parfait profiteroles with rhubarb chutney and pistachio crumb

INGREDIENTS

For the rhubarb chutney:

Dash of oil
1 large red onion, finely diced
2 garlic cloves, minced
1 thumb-sized piece fresh ginger, peeled and grated
1 tsp mustard seeds
500g rhubarb, trimmed and chopped into 2cm pieces
1 apple (Bramley ideally), peeled, cored and grated
150g soft brown sugar
½ tsp ground cloves
Generous pinch of salt
150ml cider vinegar
1 orange (zest and juice)

For the parfait:

1 shallot, diced
1 large garlic clove
1 tsp dried thyme leaves
300g chicken livers
1 tbsp brandy
300g butter
Salt and pepper

For the choux pastry:
50g butter
50g milk
50g water
Pinch of salt
100g flour
2 large eggs, whisked at room temp

To finish:
100g ground pistachio (crumb)

Method

1. Start with rhubarb chutney as can be made days/months in advance. In a heavy-bottomed saucepan, heat a dash of oil over medium heat. Add the onion and cook for 5–7 minutes until softened and translucent; don't colour it. Add the garlic, ginger and mustard seeds, and stir for 1 minute until fragrant.
2. Add the rhubarb, apple, sugar, cloves and salt, and stir until coated. Pour in the cider vinegar and orange juice, and add zest. Bring to a gentle boil, then reduce to a low simmer and cook for 45 minutes until thick and glossy. Adjust the sweet/sour balance, then cool.
3. Parfait base. Prep the livers by trimming the membranes and any green bits. Pat completely dry. Sweat the shallot, garlic and thyme in a pan with a knob of butter until soft.
4. Cook the livers. In the same pan, add another knob of butter and cook livers gently until just firm but still tender. Deglaze with brandy and bubble for 2–3 minutes. Blitz in a food processor.
5. Mount with butter. Let the liver mix cool slightly before

adding the softened butter in thirds, blending until silky smooth. Season well and pass through a chinois. Place into piping bag, chill in fridge to set.

6. On to the choux base. In a saucepan over a medium-high heat, add the butter, milk, water and salt, and bring to a scald (just shy of boiling). Add the flour and beat hard with wooden spoon, then cook out for 4–5 minutes on a lower heat until it forms a smooth ball. Tip it into a bowl to cool slightly.
7. While still warm (not hot), add the egg gradually until you get a loose, mash consistency that holds shape but drops slowly from the spoon. Put into a piping bag.
8. Bake profiteroles. Heat the oven to 180°C fan. Stick the parchment down with small dots of choux under the corners. Pipe ping-pong-sized rounds, leaving space, and dab the choux tops with a wet finger. Bake for 25 minutes until risen and golden. Turn the oven off and leave inside for 10–15 minutes to dry out. Cool.
9. Assemble. Fill the profiteroles with the parfait by poking a small hole and piping in (or split and spoon). Finish by dipping the tops of the filled profiteroles in rhubarb chutney, then pistachio crumb. Serve.

Cow-arse pie

Ingredients

1.5–2kg ox cheek
Salt and pepper
Dash of oil
Flour for dusting
Dash of brandy
200g pancetta
3 large shallots, finely chopped
1 large carrot, finely diced
2 celery sticks, finely diced
4 garlic cloves, grated
1 tbsp tomato purée
Large bouquet garni (thyme, rosemary, 2 bay leaves)
300ml full-bodied red wine
400ml veal stock
1 tin chopped tomatoes
2 tbsp Dijon mustard
2 tsp Worcestershire sauce
1 parmesan rind
200g beurre manié (100g butter and 100g flour mixed to paste)
Optional gastrique to finish seasoning
500g shortcrust pastry

1 large egg, whisked
1 tbsp double cream
1 large bone marrow

Method

1. Prep the cheeks. Trim away any thick or stringy fat from the protein, then season generously with salt and black pepper. Heat a Dutch oven or heavy pot over a high heat with a dash of oil.
2. Dust the cheeks in a coat of flour before searing in batches until deep brown on all sides. Set aside. Deglaze the pan with a splash of brandy, scraping up every last bit of caramelised goodness.
3. Turn the heat down to medium and add the pancetta. The aim is not to brown, but to slowly render and release smoky fat for about 10 minutes. Add the shallots, carrot and celery and sweat further until soft and fragrant, then add the garlic and tomato purée and cook it out for 1–2 minutes until it slightly darkens.
4. Pour in the red wine, crank the heat and let it bubble furiously for a minute to burn off the alcohol. Add the stock, bouquet garni, tomatoes and parmesan rind, and stir.
5. Slow and low. Return the ox cheeks to the pot, making sure they're submerged. Cover tight and cook either on the hob at low-medium or in the oven at 140°C for around 4 hours until the meat pulls apart with a fork.
6. Reduce and enrich. Remove the cheeks and tear gently into shreds. Fish out the bouquet garni and parmesan rind. Ladle out about half the liquid into a separate pan, whisk in the Dijon mustard and Worcestershire sauce, and reduce

over high heat until thick and glossy. Fold back through the meat, then stir through beurre manié. Season, taste and adjust with gastrique if needed. Cool completely then refrigerate until needed.

7. Assemble. When ready to bake, preheat oven to 180°C. Pack the cooled braised cheeks into pie dish.
8. On a floured surface roll out the pastry. Place the up-facing bone marrow in the centre of the rolled-out pastry, marking the spot and cutting a neat hole for the bone to poke through.
9. Seal the deal. Fit the pastry lid over the pie dish holding the filling, pressing carefully to edge out any pockets of air, and seal snugly around the marrow bone that's standing into the meat filling. Crimp the edges with a fork, brush generously with egg and cream wash, and bake for 30–45 minutes until crust is burnished gold and audibly crisp.
10. Rest briefly before serving. The marrow will have rendered into the pie beneath.

Lobster bisque

Ingredients

3 medium-large live lobsters
Oil (for roasting the shells)
Butter (for roasting the shells and finishing the lobster)
3 medium shallots, chopped
½ bulb fennel, chopped
2 carrots, diced
2 celery ribs, diced
3 cloves garlic
Flat-leaf parsley stalks
3 sprigs thyme
2 bay leaf
1 tbsp tomato purée
Small pinch of cayenne pepper
Splash of brandy
200ml white wine
500ml fish stock
500ml chicken stock
400ml double cream
Sea salt
100g cold butter cubes (to finish the bisque)
Brandy butter/crème fraîche
Tarragon and chives to finish

Method

1. Take a breath, find some zen and kill your lobsters. Point a sturdy knife between the eyes and press with purpose. Twist off the claws and tail after killing.
2. Steam/poach the claws and tails for 1–2 minutes until the shells start to turn bright red. This isn't to fully cook; it's just enough to remove the flesh cleanly. Take the meat out and chill in a tray for later. Crush all the shells and body with a mallet until well broken up.
3. Roast shells. In a roasting tray, place the crushed shells with a generous amount of oil (enough to cover but not swimming). Under a medium-high heat, grill them until they sear and smell toasted. A real dark-rouge colour is key.
4. Sauté vegetables. Add the shallots, carrots, fennel, celery and garlic in a large pot (one in which your lobsters and stock will need to fit). Turn the heat to medium and cook until lightly browned, stirring so they don't stick. Add parsley, thyme and bay and cook for 5 minutes more.
5. Stir in the tomato purée and cayenne. Cook out for 2–3 minutes until the paste darkens and loses its raw acidity.
6. Deglaze. Add brandy and white wine, and flambé carefully to burn off the alcohol, then reduce slightly. Take out your charred lobster shells from the grill and add them to the pot, along with the fish and chicken stock. Bring to a boil and season with a couple of generous pinches of salt. Drop to a simmer and cook for 1–2 hours, stirring occasionally and skimming any scum.
7. Strain. Pass the whole mix through a fine chinois so you just have your liquid gold. Reserve 2 ladles of cooked veg and put to the side. Discard the rest.

8. Finish the bisque. Blend until smooth, adding your reserved veg and cream while doing so. You want to coat the back of a spoon, but not loose enough to not be a sauce. Pass through a chinois one final time for supreme silkiness. Keep warm (but don't boil).
9. Thicken with butter. Whisk/blend in cold butter cubes, a little at a time, until glossy and rich. Taste and adjust seasoning.
10. Lobster. Take lobster out of fridge and slice the meat into bite-size chunks. Season, then sauté in butter on a hot pan just to finish meat to cooked.
11. Serve. Plate the bisque, add the lobster chunks and finish with a quenelle of brandy butter or crème fraîche, plus fresh tarragon and chives.

Lapin à la moutarde avec escargots (rabbit in mustard with snails)

Ingredients

For the rabbit:

1 whole rabbit, jointed
Salt and pepper
Neutral oil
100g butter
2 large shallots
1 tbsp flour
200ml dry white wine
150g chicken stock
Half a dozen thyme sprigs, tied
2 bay leaves
3 tbsp Dijon mustard (keep 1 tbsp back for finishing)
200g double cream
1 tbsp crème fraîche
Lemon zest
Micro herbs and parsley to finish

For the escargots:

1 medium can cooked snails (200–250g)
200g butter
50g parsley leaves (trimmed from stem, chopped)
3 large cloves garlic

1 tsp white wine vinegar
Heavy pinch of sea salt
Olive oil to loosen
2 tbsp breadcrumbs

Method

1. Take the rabbit out of the fridge and let it loose to unchill (1 hour minimum). Season well with salt and pepper – not politely, but properly. Heat some neutral oil in a heavy pot or Dutch oven over a medium-high heat and brown the rabbit (in batches if needed) and baste with a good helping of butter in the pan when starting to colour (approx. 2 tbsps). Keep an eye out so the butter doesn't burn. You want a golden colour all round, not steamed beige. Pull the rabbit out and park on a tray.
2. Drop the heat slightly and throw in your shallots, along with another helping of butter. Let them soften for 5 mintues and go sweet. Stir in the flour and cook it out for a minute. It will go grainy, but persevere.
3. Splash in the wine and let it boil hard for a minute, scraping up every stuck-on bit. Add the chicken stock, thyme, bay leaf and 2 tbsp of Dijon mustard. Season. Stir. Smell.
4. Nestle the rabbit back into the pot. Bring just up to a boil, then drop the heat low, put lid on and let it gently mutter for about 1 hour until tender.
5. Make the garlic butter for the snails. Put the butter, parsley, vinegar, garlic and salt into a food processor and whizz thoroughly. Add a splash of olive oil if needed to loosen. Once green, smooth and combined, scoop it into a piping bag and set aside.

6. Remove the snails from can and rinse in a sieve, discarding any slime or juice. Pat dry, then place into escargot pan/muffin tin/small tray. Pipe a large blob of butter over each snail and refrigerate.
7. When the rabbit is tender, remove the meat to the side. Turn the heat up high and reduce the sauce by half. Add the double cream and crème fraîche. Put the rabbit back in and warm through gently, but don't boil. Now whisk in the remaining Dijon mustard and lemon zest at the end for punch. Taste and adjust seasoning.
8. Put the snails topped with the garlic butter under the grill on high. Once melted and starting to colour, take them out to sprinkle over the breadcrumbs. Return them to the grill for the breadcrumbs to turn toasted brown. Don't look away: it will only take seconds.
9. Plate up 2 cuts of lapin per serving, with a spoonful of mustard sauce, micro herbs and parsley. Place your little green escargots around the crevices and nooks of the rabbit cuts to finish.

Scallop tortellini with roe beurre blanc, caviar and crackling

INGREDIENTS

For the roe butter:

Scallop roe from the muscles, cleaned
120g cold unsalted butter, cubed
Salt
Dash of lemon/olive oil
1 garlic clove
Lemon juice/olive oil to loosen

For the scallop filling:

150g fresh scallops, cleaned (muscle only)
30ml crème fraîche
70ml double cream
Zest of ½ lemon
Pepper
Pinch of salt
Extra 2 scallops for texture

For the pasta dough:

250g flour plus extra for dusting
2 large eggs
1 egg yolk

Pinch of salt
Semolina (for dusting)

For the roe beurre blanc:
1 shallot, diced
300ml dry white wine (not cooking wine)
1 tbsp white wine vinegar
Lemon thyme
Lemon juice to taste
Salt to taste

To finish:
Chives, finely sliced
Roe eggs (beluga or trout depending on client)

Option for pork garnish:
Crackling/pancetta/crispy Parma ham/black pudding

Method

1. Start with scallops. The key here is to try to keep everything a cool temp. Firstly remove the orange roe from the muscle to make the roe butter; you want just the orange coral. Blend them in a food processor with 120g butter, garlic, salt and dash of lemon/olive oil to loosen. Chill in fridge.
2. Roughly chop the scallop muscle, then blitz with crème fraîche, double cream, lemon zest, salt and pepper. You're after a smooth mousse texture, not gluey. Taste, adjust the seasoning and chill in a piping bag.
3. On to the pasta dough. Combine the flour, eggs, yolk and salt (using either the well method or a food processor – I choose the latter). Wrap tight and rest at room

temperature for 30 minutes. Then knead for 8–10 minutes until smooth and elastic. Wrap again and rest for 15 more minutes before rolling.

4. Roll and shape the tortellini. Have a bowl of flour on station to use on the dough as you go. Roll the pasta thin enough so you can just about read through it, then cut it into 8cm circles. Prepare a small bowl of water for sealing the tortellini, along with a tray dusted generously with semolina for the end product.
5. Pipe a small marble-sized amount of filling into the centre of the tortellini cut-out as well as 4–5 chopped chunks of the fresh scallop for depth of texture. Wet one half of the rim, fold into a half moon and press out any air. Bring the corners together around a circular tool (a steel knife sharpener is ideal) and pinch to form tortellini, before placing into the semolina-dusted tray. Keep in mind that this is raw shellfish and it can be a long technique, so keep the batches refrigerated and not sitting out for too long.
6. Roe beurre blanc. Put shallot, wine, vinegar and lemon thyme into a saucepan and turn the heat up until reduced to a super-concentrated liquid of just a few tablespoons. Strain and return the liquid to the pan.
7. Lower the heat to medium-low and whisk in cold roe butter, cube by cube, keeping it glossy and emulsified. Do not boil or it will split. Taste and season with lemon juice and salt. It should be an orange custard-like consistency that coats the back of your spoon.
8. Cook the tortellini in well-salted water just shy of boiling for 1–2 minutes (they float when tender). Plate 4–6 tortellini into each bowl and coat with the roe beurre blanc. Finish with chives, a small quenelle of caviar and shards of crispy pork skin/variant, if using.

Cherry frangipane tart

INGREDIENTS

For the jam:

250g cherries, washed, pitted and halved
125g caster sugar
1 lemon (zest and juice)
Splash of water

For the pastry:

250g plain white flour
150g unsalted butter, cold diced
80g icing sugar, sifted
2 egg yolks
Pinch of salt

For the frangipane and filling:

250g butter, softened
250g caster sugar
2 eggs
250g ground almonds
70g polenta
2 vanilla pods (or vanilla paste/extract)
12 ripe cherries, pitted and halved

To finish:
Sugar syrup (for glaze)
Crème fraîche

Method

1. Jam. Add the cherries, sugar, lemon juice and zest, and a splash of water to a small pot. Bring to a boil, then reduce to a simmer. Stir for 10 minutes until thick and consistent. Cool.
2. Pastry. Pulse the flour and cold diced butter in a food processor until it resembles coarse breadcrumbs. Add the sifted icing sugar, egg yolks and a pinch of salt, and mix until it clumps and pulls from the sides. Wrap and fridge for 1 hour.
3. Base. Heat oven to 160°C fan. Coarsely grate pastry into a 30cm loose-bottom tart tin. Press evenly around the base and sides. Spread a generous layer of cooled jam on the base and chill.
4. Frangipane. Add the softened butter, caster sugar, eggs, ground almonds, polenta and vanilla into food processor and pulse until combined. It should take the loose consistency of hummus.
5. Build and bake. Pour the frangipane into the pastry shell (about two-thirds full). Arrange the cherry halves, starting on the outside and working inwards. Bake for around 1 hour until the frangipane is set and going golden brown.
6. Finish. Cool fully, then brush with sugar syrup for glaze. Serve with crème fraîche.

Salted dark chocolate and ginger brownie with candied pecans and whipped cardamom mascarpone

INGREDIENTS

For the brownie:

250g butter
300g dark chocolate (70 or 80 per cent)
300g dark cooking chocolate (Bournville)
80g peeled ginger, finely chopped
300g sugar
5 eggs
Sea salt

For the candied pecans:

100g caster sugar
2 tbsp water
200g pecans

For the whipped mascarpone:

500g mascarpone
2 tbsp double cream
1 tbsp icing sugar
½ tsp finely ground cardamom

Method

1. Turn the oven on to 180°C fan. Line a medium-sized baking tray with baking parchment and butter it.
2. Melt the butter and both chocolates together in a bain-marie over a medium heat (give the butter a couple of minutes' head start so you don't burn the chocolate). Once melted and smooth, stir in the chopped ginger and take off the heat.
3. While melting, beat the sugar and eggs in a separate bowl with an electric whisk until the mix expands roughly three times in size and goes pale.
4. Let the chocolate mix cool a minute, then pour into the egg and sugar, and whisk until fully combined.
5. Pour the batter into lined tray. Sprinkle the surface lightly with sea salt and bake for 20 minutes at 180°C fan (or until the centre is no longer wet when poked with a knife). Cool completely before slicing.
6. Candied pecans. In a small pot, add the caster sugar and water. Heat gently, stirring to dissolve, then turn up to medium-high until you've got a slow bubbling syrup (careful not to brown).
7. Lightly oil a sheet of parchment. Add the pecans to the syrup and stir to coat. Tip onto the oiled parchment and separate with tongs while hot. Leave to harden.
8. Whipped mascarpone. Beat the mascarpone by itself first until creamy and smooth, then add small amounts of double cream just to loosen, along with the icing sugar and cardamom for about a minute until velvety (don't overwhip; if it's grainy, start again).
9. Serve the brownie in long, elegant rectangles. Pipe or quenelle whipped mascarpone on top and finish with candied pecans.

Acknowledgements

A huge thanks to the following:

Sabhbh Curran – agent
Sara Cywinski – publisher
Laura Carr – managing editorial director
Kimberley Nyamhondera – head of publicity
Emma Pidsley – jacket designer
Lindsay Nash and Clare Sivell – text designers
Holly Sheldrake – senior production manager
Becky Lushey – senior marketing manager
Jiri Greco – editorial assistant
Nige Tassell – copy-editor
James Nightingale – proofreader